CONTRIBUTIONS TO THE HISTORY OF NORTH AMERICAN NATURAL HISTORY

Papers from the First North American Conference
of the
Society for the Bibliography of Natural History
held at
The Academy of Natural Sciences,
Philadelphia,
21–23 October 1981

Edited by Alwyne Wheeler

Published by the Society for the Bibliography of Natural History
(Society for the Bibliography of Natural History Special Publication
Number 2.)

London
1983

Published by the Society for the Bibliography of Natural History
c/o British Museum (Natural History)
Cromwell Road,
London SW7 5BD

© Society for the Bibliography of Natural History
April 1983

ISBN 0 90 184305 9

HOBBS THE PRINTERS LIMITED · MILLBROOK
SOUTHAMPTON SO9 2UZ

CONTENTS

INTRODUCTION

It was fitting that the first North American Conference of the Society for the Bibliography of Natural History was held at the Academy of Natural Sciences in Philadelphia; for Philadelphia is the cradle of the study of American natural history. (The Academy even faces Logan Circle named for James Logan who was an early American physiological botanist.) Philadelphia was the home of such eminent scientists as the Bartrams, Benjamin Franklin, the Peale family, Benjamin Rush, David Rittenhouse, Caspar Wistar, and Samuel Rafinesque. The scientific activities of the young America were centered in Philadelphia, which was the capital until 1800 and the country's largest city. Many of the great scientific societies and institutions were founded here in the early years of this country: the Library Company (1731), the American Philosphical Society (1743), the College of Physicians (1787), the Peale Museum (1784), and the Academy of Natural Sciences (1812).

The conference was the first opportunity for the North American membership to come together to discuss mutual interests. It was an opportune time to hold such a conference to discuss North American contributions to the history and bibliography of natural history, for it is only in the last decade or so that we have begun to look back and view our heritage with an historical perspective. Until recently we have been busy defining borders, exploring and settling our land, surveying our resources, gathering and cataloging collections, and developing our cultural institutions. Now we are ready to look at our history, collections, and institutions with some amount of objectivity.

The papers and discussions of this first North American conference of the Society for the Bibliography of Natural History reflect this historical interest in our continent, as well as a concern for the continuing development of the bibliography and history of North American natural sciences. We look at our host institution, the Academy of Natural Sciences, travel along the Bartram trail, visit with Thomas Say and François-André Michaux at New Harmony, share the experience of compiling an historic geology bibliography, trek with Titian R. Peale, John Gould, and Thomas Coulter, and venture north into Hudson's Bay. The three panel discussions, that are not transcribed in these proceedings, considered the imperfections, needs and future of American natural history bibliography. Panel I, Scientists and Practitioners, was moderated by Richard Van Gelder, American Museum of Natural History, included Valerie Monkhouse, of the National Museums of Canada, Robert Armstrong, Longwood Gardens, James Atz, American Museum of Natural History, Robert Hazen, Carnegie Institution, Eleanor McLean, Blacker-Wood Library, McGill University, Elizabeth Zipf, Biosciences Information Services, and Bernadette Callery, Hunt Institute. Panel II, Collectors and Antiquarian Booksellers, included Philip Weimerskirch, Burndy Library, Edwin Wolf II, The Library Company, Lee Ash, Library Consultant, Estelle Chassid, The Book Chest, Donald Creswell, W. Graham Arader III, Howell J. Heaney, The Free Library, and Elizabeth Woodburn, Booknoll Farm. Panel III, Publishers, Editors, and Current Booksellers included Dana J. Pratt, Library of Congress, Charles Gruchy, National Museums of Canada,

Maurice English, University of Pennsylvania Press, Harry Luprecht, bookseller and publisher, and Marjorie Shaw, San Diego Zoo.

The three panels discussed Natural History Bibliography: Imperfections, Urgent Needs, and Prospects for Betterment. Panel I approached the problem from the point of view of Scientists and Practitioners of the art and heard opinions that hard work, diligence, accuracy, and perseverance, as underpinnings of scholarship are still necessary basics in spite of the advantages of modern computer technology. Indeed, as financing resources become more sparse in the present economy, they must be emphasized as the select elements supporting bibliographical methodologies.

Panel II looked at the theme as Collectors and Antiquarian Booksellers, and learned of the urgency for better descriptive cataloging (since the rise in number of home booksellers), especially with regard to the collation and physical description of the condition of materials, and heard also that the rising market price for useful and important books of natural history was continuing [and does so still, Summer 1982]. George Lowry, Swann Galleries, explained the working of the American auction market and brought forth many questions from the interested audience.

Panel III Publishers, Editors, and Current [Trade] Booksellers, was a practical learning session for the audience, which consisted largely of a body of potential authors. The practical problems of publishers and editors seeking new publishable manuscripts—and the factors that must be in balance before their acceptance (competitiveness, cost, levels of scholarship/readership, sales potential, and booklife) were described. This was followed by bookseller's explanations of the very limited profit and sales likelihood of all but the most popular-type of book with readership appeal.

Gratitude and appreciation must be expressed to the Program Committee, Lee Ash, Valerie Monkhouse, Marjorie Shaw, and Charles Gruchy, for their hard work, imaginative program, and the excellent speakers and panelists they invited. Sylva Baker and Thomas Peter Bennett deserve special thanks for hosting the Conference, for the exceptional hospitality accorded the participants by the Academy, and for all the local arrangements. We are grateful to the Free Library of Philadelphia, the College of Physicians, The Library Company, and the American Philosophical Society for their hospitality. The walking tour to these citadels of natural history collections was one of the highlights of the Conference. In driving rain, no one faltered, and all continued from one library to the next, fearful of missing a glimpse of a rare manuscript or object.

And most of all thanks are due to the speakers who prepared such excellent papers and to the panelists who gave thoughtful presentations.

Nina J. Root
American Museum of Natural History

THE HISTORY OF THE ACADEMY OF NATURAL SCIENCES OF PHILADELPHIA

Thomas Peter Bennett
President, The Academy of Natural Sciences,
19th and the Parkway,
Philadelphia,
Pennsylvania 19103

Any discussion of the past, present, and future of the Academy of Natural Sciences of Philadelphia must begin by my pointing out that future historians will note that the Society for Bibliography of Natural History gathered at the Academy of Natural Sciences of Philadelphia in their first meeting on this continent in October, 1981.

During much of the nineteenth and twentieth centuries in the Americas, the Academy of Natural Sciences had functioned at the cutting edge of innovation in scientific inquiry. The history of the Academy parallels the development of scientific inquiry in America and thus involves the emergence of first the serious amateur and then the professional as students of natural history. The Academy's role as catalyst was perhaps first recorded by the eminent malacologist Dr Amos Binney, who in 1851 dedicated his three-volume monograph, *The terrestrial air-breathing mollusks of the United States*, with these words:

> To the Academy of Natural Sciences of Philadelphia, to whose founders is due the first effective impulse given to the study of natural science of North America, and whose labors have been mainly instrumental in developing the natural history of this country.

At the beginning of the nineteenth century Philadelphia, the largest and most prosperous city in America, boasted many of the leading scientific organizations in this new country: a sampling includes the Library Company, the American Philosophical Society, Bartram's Botanic Garden, as well as the private observatory of David Rittenhouse and Charles Willson Peale's Museum of Natural History. The American Philosophical Society held a distinguished position in the world of scholarship and its membership ranks were filled with those who were well-established in their scientific accomplishments. Public interest in science was great. Peale's Museum drew crowds to view its impressive collections of animal specimens (particularly birds) and fossils such as the "mammoth"; natural curiosities were also displayed at the Library Company or added to collections at the American Philosophical Society and the College of Physicians and Surgeons.

Natural history was at home in the new democratic republic and, as Daniel Boorstin noted in *The Americans*, ". . . new knowledge which life in America made possible, precisely because it was factual and miscellaneous, required no preliminary training. One could plunge in anywhere. Knowledge of the

Contributions to the History of North American Natural History. Society for the Bibliography of Natural History, London, 1983.

Figure 1. The Artist in his Museum by Charles Willson Peale. (Pennsylvania Academy of Fine Arts.)

New World—its climate, geography, plants, animals, savages and diseases—
was accessible to everyone . . . The casual report of the course of a river
was a piece of natural history . . .''.

For young persons interested in the natural sciences, however—for those
who were by day tradesmen, artisans or mechanics, physicians, merchants,
apprentices and the like, but who occupied their leisure hours with scientific
inquiry and discussion, there were few available libraries, few collections or
cabinets of specimens open for study and examination, few appropriate
locations for group meetings and prolonged discourse.

In Philadelphia several protégés of Peale and of John Bartram, along with
other young men interested in the emerging physical sciences of geology and
chemistry, apparently felt the pressing need for a younger society or association than then existed in the city, one that would permit them to meet and
share scientific information and specimens as well as develop a library for
common use. In 1812, through their efforts, the Academy of Natural Sciences
of Philadelphia was founded. Initially it was a society of persons interested
in the natural sciences, not unlike the well-established American Philosophical
Society; later it was to fulfill Peale's early ideals and objectives for his public
museum. Unfortunately, the founding of the Academy has not been subjected
to detailed scholarly scrutiny. The subject merits further examination.

Briefly, the story is this. Early in 1812, apothecary John Speakman
suggested to Jacob Gilliams, a leading Philadelphia dentist, that "if their
associates could come together at stated times where they would be free from
interruption and could compare notes as to what they supposed they knew,
they would secure more pleasure and profit than by desultory talk."[2]

Shortly after this conversation, a meeting was held in John Speakman's
rooms above his apothecary's shop on the northeast corner of High (now
Market) and Second Streets, Philadelphia. Included in this gathering were
physicians Gerard Troost (also interested in chemistry, geology, and mineralogy) and Camillus McMahon Mann along with John Shinn, Jr, manufacturing
chemist; Nicholas S. Parmentier, distiller and a manufacturer of spermaceti
oil; and Jacob Gilliams. Mr Speakman served as chairman; Dr Mann,
secretary. The minutes note: "A meeting of gentlemen, friends of science
and of rational disposure of leisure moments held by mutual concurrence
and desire at the house of John Speakman."[3]

It was agreed that the exclusive object of the new society they wished to
form should be the cultivation of the natural sciences:

. . . to form, constitute and become a Society for the purpose of occupying
their leisure . . . on subjects of NATURAL SCIENCE, interesting and useful
to the country and the world, and in model conducive to the general and
individual satisfaction of the members, as well as to the primary object
the advancement and diffusion of useful liberal human knowledge. . . .[3]

At its founding, the Academy had listed as its purposes the formation of
a natural history museum, a library of works of science, a chemical laboratory,
and a collection of experimental philosophical apparatus for the illustration
and advancement of knowledge to "the common benefit of all individuals
who may be admitted members of our institution".[3]

Figure 2. The Academy's first home over Speakman's Apothecary Shop.
(Academy of Natural Sciences.)

Figure 3. Thomas Say by Charles Willson Peale. (Academy of Natural Sciences.)

Thomas Say (later termed "Father of American Conchology" and "Father of American Entomology") although unable to attend the founding meeting was also listed as a founder. All the founders had a strong interest in the natural sciences, yet Thomas Say may be regarded as the sole "professional" naturalist of the group.

The financial constraints under which the Academy and other similar not-for-profit institutions functioned early encouraged the Academy to become community-oriented in its programs. Heavy involvement in the sciences by amateurs also suggested this direction. Popular activities responded to public curiosity in terms of objects exhibited and echoed a prevailing spirit of optimism about education and its benefits. From the beginning, however, a strong sense of scientific commitment and integrity prevailed at the Academy, paralleled by an aversion to the entertainment, or quasi-theatrical, aspects of Peale's Museum as it struggled with finances in the decades before its demise.

The requirements for membership in the Academy of Natural Sciences of Philadelphia were that one be recommended by an active member, and voted upon by the existing membership. The practice of philosophical societies was followed in having membership categories for residents and non-residents. Resident members paid dues, and they alone could vote, but contributions to the cabinets and library were encouraged from corresponding members as well, as were papers for presentation at meeting or publication in the Academy's *Journal* (begun in 1817).

With no limit on term of office, the Academy like other societies developed a core group of dedicated resident members who directed local activities. George Ord, for many years Vice President, was one such example: an antagonist of John James Audubon, he and fellow members blocked Audubon's election to membership for years.[4] On the other hand, an influential correspondent of the Academy, Thomas Jefferson, was instrumental in helping focus on fossils from Big Bone Lick, Kentucky which subsequently became part of the Academy's collections—although in his letter accepting membership Jefferson dismissed the importance of his own efforts.[5]

Although several societies for the study of natural history had been organized in America before 1812 and had attempted to concentrate the scientific talent and enterprise of naturalists in forming museums, both "amateur" and those more "professional", they proved ephemeral. For reasons that historians must yet detail, the Academy remained the exception in the early nineteenth century. By 1814 its growth in members, books, and specimens was already such that plans were laid to move to larger quarters to accommodate the burgeoning collections and library. In 1815 the Academy leased a hall, a new, three-storey building with the second and third floors to be used by the library and museum, the ground floor for laboratory space, in Gilliams' Court, off Arch Street, a short distance from Speakman's shop. In 1826 the Academy acquired the first property to which it had full title, at the southeast corner of Philadelphia's 12th and Sansom Streets. The bulk of the associated expense was met by wealthy merchant and amateur of science William Maclure, who served as President from 1817 until 1840. Maclure had noted that "all inquiry into the nature and property of rocks, or the

Figure 4. William Maclure by Charles Willson Peale. (Academy of Natural Sciences.)

relative situations they occupy on the surface of the earth, has been much neglected"; his *Observations on the Geology of the United States;with some remarks on the effect produced on the nature and fertility of soils, by the decomposition of the different classes of rocks* (1817) represents the first major geological examination of the North American continent.

Peale's Museum and the Academy of Natural Sciences paralleled each other in the growth of their collections. By 1822, the year following completion of the famous self-portrait of Peale in his Museum, the Academy's collections already surpassed those of Peale's Museum, except for Peale's collection of birds. Peale's bird department, the largest and most complete collection in his Museum, served as a major resource for Alexander Wilson when he was writing his *American Ornithology*. Wilson referred to specimens in Peale's Museum, citing their catalogue numbers so that others would have a "type specimen" to associate with the description and plate in his work. After he became a member of the Academy in 1813, many of his type specimens became part of the Academy's collections, where they are still to be found today. The ninth and last volume of *American Ornithology* was completed after Wilson's death by Academy Vice President George Ord and Academy member Charles Lucien Bonaparte and contained plates by the 17-year-old Titian Ramsay Peale II (soon to become a member).[6]

By mid-nineteenth century, the Academy was recognised as the best-equipped institution in America for the study of the natural sciences; its library holdings in particular were rich.

Membership figures were equally noteworthy. The original seven had grown to approximately 200 living members; there were an additional 450 or more corresponding members. Qualitative growth matched quantitative growth: of the 55 most prolific contributors to national American scientific journals between 1815 and 1845, 44 (80%) were affiliated with the Academy of Natural Sciences.

Even a brief listing of the active and corresponding members of the Academy during this period is impressive, for it includes most of the magisterial figures of the time in natural sciences. Among the active (that is, local) members of note were George Ord, Thomas Say, Alexander Wilson, Benjamin H. Coates, Zacchaeus Collins, Reuben Haines, Richard Harlan, Augustus E. Jessup, William H. Keating, Isaac Lea, Charles A. Lesueur, Titian Ramsay Peale II, Lardner Vanuxem. Distinguished correspondents who were elected during this period include J. J. Audubon, William Bartram, Baron George Cuvier, Thomas Jefferson, Pierre Andre Latreille, Chevalier de Lamarck, Maj. Stephen H. Long. F. A. Michaux, Thomas Nuttall, C. S. Rafinesque, and Benjamin Silliman.

In the 1870s, to arrive at a new home in time for America's Centennial celebrations, the Academy of Natural Sciences again moved its headquarters, this time to a new structure at 19th and Race Streets on Logan Square;

This was the era of the great Joseph Leidy. Born in Philadelphia in 1823, Leidy was first an artist whose talent was developed during his youth and was later reflected in the accuracy and beauty of his drawings of microscopic objects. As a faculty member at the University of Pennsylvania, where he

Figure 5. Alexander Wilson by Charles Willson Peale. (American Philosophical Society.)

Figure 6. 1876 building, Academy of Natural Sciences. (Academy of Natural Sciences.)

Figure 7. Joseph Leidy as a young man. (Academy of Natural Sciences.)

taught anatomy and ultimately became Professor, Leidy did research at the Academy in paleontology and parasitology. (This was common at the time; M.D.s practiced and taught for pay at the medical schools in Philadelphia and did their research at the Academy, where they were often members of one of its departments.) Leidy's first major contribution to science was in parasitology, his most important work being *A Fauna and Flora within Living Animals* (1853).

However, while Leidy was studying parasites, he was also starting a revolution in American paleontology which, prior to his work, was limited to investigation of scattered fossil "curiosities" of unknown origin. His active involvement for a quarter of a century transformed this pattern. In 1847 he proved the existence of fossil horses in America and traced the lineage of the horse and other hoofed animals; in 1858 he supervised the excavation of the first dinosaur (*Hadrosaurus foulkii*) found in America.[7]

Leidy avoided becoming embroiled in the dispute in which Asa Gray defended Darwin against the attacks of Louis Agassiz. A frequent correspondent with Darwin, Leidy did however recommend Darwin's membership in Academy of Natural Sciences and with Leidy's support Darwin was elected in 1859, his first election to an American scholarly society after publication of *The Origin of the Species*.

Despite Leidy's key role in the development of scientific inquiry in America, and the international tributes paid to him on the centenary of his birth, no definitive biographical study of Leidy has been published (preliminary biographical manuscripts and extensive archival materials await interested scholars in the Academy's library). Other important Academy holdings of value to modern historians of science include correspondence by the botanist Constantin Rafinesque; letters and drawings of Jacob Cist; and papers of the entomologist S. S. Haldeman, botanist L. D. de Schweinitz, conchologists Thomas Say and Isaac Lea. Also of interest are the collections of papers from the innumerable local natural history societies active in this area during the nineteenth century.

A number of prominent figures have been associated with scientific research at the Academy in the post-Leidy period. The Academy can point with considerable pride to the contributions made by the great Henry Pilsbry and by G. W. Tryon in malacology; Witmer Stone, James Bond, and Rodolphe de Shauensee in ornithology; H. Radclyffe Roberts, entomology; Samuel Gordon, mineralogy; Francis Pennell, botany; Henry Fowler, ichthyology; Edward Drinker Cope, paleontology; and, of course, Dr Ruth Patrick and the specialization of limnological studies which she instituted at the Academy in 1948 with the founding of the Division of Limnology and Ecology.

In support of the Academy's continuing interest in research in the environmental sciences the Benedict Estuarine Research Laboratory was established in 1966 in Benedict, Maryland on the Chesapeake Bay to study marshland and tidal ecologies. The Stroud Water Research Center, at Avondale, Pennsylvania, followed in 1968; here, experimental flow-through streams aid researchers in examining stream life and pollution biology. Work done at these two field facilities when coupled with research at the Philadelphia headquarters provides a unified picture of the most current scientific thinking in basic and applied research on all kinds of aquatic ecosystems, and the effects of human activity upon these ecosystems.

Late in 1976, a major $13 million construction program was undertaken by the Academy which has resulted in capital improvements to the existing Logan Square complex and construction of a new eight-level research building, auditorium facilities, the Widener Science Education Center, and Hall of Changing Exhibits. After five years, the revitalization of older education, exhibit, research, and administrative areas is complete, leaving before us the final component scheduled for restoration and expansion—the library. Planning for new library facilities is well under way, and it is anticipated that construction will begin in 1983. Thus relocations of the Academy, expansion of its holdings, and modernization of its facilities have been a process of evolution for 170 years.

Underlying the renewal of physical facilities remains the original mission of the Academy and its members, to examine, discuss, and disseminate information about the natural sciences. Today's work by the public museum and the Division of Education is an outgrowth of the early exhibits made by Academy naturalists to demonstrate objects of their study to fellow naturalists and to the public on special occasions. From these early exhibits grew the museum dioramas and the educational programs which make use of these education tools.

The Academy's scientific divisions today accomplish their mission through the study of the identity, order and relationship of organisms in order to understand the diversity of life and the biological changes in organisms; through studies in evolutionary biology which explores the dynamics of biological change, including adaptation, survival and extinction; and through studies in global ecology, which teaches man to understand the natural world so that he can develop civilizations within the constraints of natural laws.

Through its educational programs, its publications, its service to the community, its museum exhibits, its scientific research and consultation, the Academy today communicates an understanding of the wonder and excitement of the living world. It interprets natural objects and reveals their relevancy to everyday interests and experiences. It reveals the underlying principles and relationships which tie natural objects to each other in a dynamic and evolving system. It seeks to stimulate concern and responsibility toward the earth and its ecology.

NOTES AND REFERENCES

[1] Amos Binney, *The terrestrial air-breathing mollusks of the United States* . . . ed. Augustus A. Gould . . . vol. I. Boston, 1851–78.

[2] E. J. Nolan, 1909 *A short history of the Academy of Natural Sciences of Philadelphia*. Academy of Natural Sciences of Philadelphia: 5.

[3] Academy of Natural Sciences of Philadelphia, *Articles of Agreement*. January 25, 1812.

[4] Scholarly research on Audubon and his relationship to members of the Academy is sorely needed and would bring to light a number of interesting issues now only mentioned in passing, the precise nature of George Ord's involvement; whether Audubon was black-balled in his first try at membership, etc.

[5] Academy of Natural Sciences of Philadelphia, Archives. Letter from Jefferson to Reuben Haines, 18 May, 1818, copy. See also Silvio A. Bedini, 1981–82 Jefferson: Man of science, *Frontiers Annual*: Academy of Natural Sciences of Philadelphia. III: 10–24.

[6] The youngest son of Charles Willson Peale, Titian Ramsay Peale II (1799–1885) was named after his elder brother, who had died at 18. Titian was an artist-scientist, a protégé of his father and a colleague of Thomas Say, George Ord, and other members of the fledgling Academy. He was born in Philosophical Hall where his family lived as caretakers in association with Peale's Museum; he lived there for 11 years. In this setting he frequently encountered leading naturalists and artists of the time as they visited the Hall and his father's museum. In 1816, when he was only 17, he began making drawings for Thomas Say's pioneering work on American insects. This project involved his consulting with ANSP Vice President George Ord, who had undertaken completion of the ninth volume of Alexander Wilson's *Birds of America*; it also brought him in touch with eminent naturalists such as Thomas Nuttall (an Academy member who made use of our plant collections as a basis for his 1818 book about American plants).

[7] Joseph Leidy, 1847 On the Fossil Horse of America *Proceedings of the Academy of Natural Sciences of Philadelphia* 3: 262–66.

NATURAL HISTORY IN UTOPIA:
THE WORKS OF THOMAS SAY AND FRANÇOIS-ANDRÉ MICHAUX
PRINTED AT NEW HARMONY, INDIANA

Ian MacPhail
Librarian,
The Morton Arboretum,
Lisle,
Illinois 60532

On a winter's day at the end of January 1826, a shallow-bottomed keelboat (one of those indispensable workhorses of the Mississippi and its tributaries) drew up to the landing-stage at New Harmony, Indiana, on the Wabash after a long journey down the Ohio from Pittsburgh. Some of the passengers had already disembarked several days before at the Mount Vernon landing on the Ohio with the bulk of the luggage and travelled in heavy waggons overland to New Harmony but most were still on board. That long voyage down the Ohio may not rank with the voyages of the *Pinta* or the *Mayflower* but it has its own secure place in the history of science in North America. On board were some of the most illustrious figures in the intellectual life of Philadelphia. The name of the keelboat was the *Philanthropist* but someone called it "the Boatload of Knowledge" and that is the label that has come down to posterity.

Who were they and what were they doing in this mosquito-ridden village in the Indiana bush far from the elegant and gracious life of Philadelphia?

As every schoolboy knows, New Harmony, Indiana, was the scene of a famous social experiment in the early nineteenth century. The site, an old Indian camping ground on the east bank of the Wabash River had been first settled by George Rapp, a pietist preacher from Württemberg in Germany in 1814, when he and his followers set up a religious community there. They called it Harmonie and settled down to farm the land and await the millenium, which they expected hourly. In 1824 they decided to move to Pennsylvania and they sold out to the charismatic Welsh reformer, Robert Owen, who was looking for a site for his socialist Utopia in North America. In New Harmony (as it came to be called) the community that he established was a failure in social or political terms and he himself abandoned it after two years and returned to England to organize trades unions and workers' cooperatives. But that was not the end of New Harmony. It was, rather, the beginning. It may not have been the scene of either the religious or the secular millenium but it achieved a distinction which was not foreseen by George Rapp or Robert Owen. Half a century after Owen's departure this little village was a center of natural history, an intellectual suburb, as it were,

Contributions to the History of North American Natural History. Society for the Bibliography of Natural History, London, 1983.

of Philadelphia or an anteroom of the Academy of Natural Sciences, and the place of imprint of some major works.

New Harmony was already quite crowded, with about a thousand inhabitants (it scarcely has more today), when Robert Owen, with his cajoling Welsh tongue recruited to his visionary community the thirty-odd scientists and educators from Philadelphia who comprised the "Boatload of Knowledge". Owen's second son, William, protested that what they needed most were mechanics and manual laborers, not intellectuals (that perennial cry of revolutionaries) but, in fact, as another commentator has pointed out, "if the Boatload of Knowledge had not come to New Harmony, Robert Owen's social experiment in America would have received a much smaller place in history and the 'Golden Age' of cultural achievements in the village on the Wabash during the next fifty years would not have been realized".

The key figure in the flowering of natural history that ensued was undoubtedly William Maclure, the rich Scottish philanthropist, who had his own ideas of education and was looking for somewhere to put them into practice.

Maclure was born in Ayrshire in Scotland in 1763, and made a fortune as a young man in an Anglo-American mercantile firm. He had two passions: geology and the education of the young according to the system of Pestalozzi and Fellenberg. He undertook a geological survey of the United States beginning in 1796 from the Atlantic to the Rocky Mountains and from the St Lawrence to the Gulf of Mexico "crossing the dividing lines of the principal formations" as he wrote "in fifteen or twenty different places". From this he published *Observations on the geology of the United States* with a colored map, first in 1809, in revised form in 1817, a foundational work in American geology. He was an early member of the Academy of Natural Sciences and its President from 1817 until his death. When he boarded the *Philanthropist* for the journey to New Harmony he was 62 years old. He had met Owen in Scotland and was moderately interested in his ideas but it was the enthusiasm for them of others at Philadelphia that persuaded him to throw in his lot with Owen at New Harmony.

When Owen lost interest in New Harmony in 1827, Maclure became the guiding spirit of the community, though from a distance. The climate of southwest Indiana did not suit him and he spent most of his time in Mexico. His wealth supported the cultural and industrial needs of the community and his plans for it were carried out by a remarkable and energetic Frenchwoman, who acted as a sort of agent, nurse, village mayor, and earth-mother. Her name was Marie Louise Duclos Fretageot. She was a Pestalozzian teacher from Paris who had set up a seminary for young ladies of good breeding in Philadelphia at Maclure's instigation. She had been persuaded by Owen to join the experiment in New Harmony and, what was more astonishing, to bring some of her young protégées with her. What we know of the life and affairs of New Harmony between the years 1826 and 1833 comes in no small part from the voluminous correspondence that Madame Fretageot conducted with William Maclure during those years, a correspondence that is preserved and well cared for by the Library of the Workingmen's Institute in New Harmony, founded by Maclure in 1838. It is to this Library and its Librarian,

Aline Cook, that I am indebted for permission to quote the letters that follow.

Besides William Maclure and Madame Fretageot and her young ladies who else was among the Boatload of Knowledge? The most notable was Thomas Say, zoologist, entomologist, conchologist, a charter member of the Academy of Natural Sciences and Curator of the American Philosophical Society. Thomas Say had published two volumes of his *American entomology* before coming to New Harmony. The third was published while he was there. In New Harmony he was to produce the *American conchology* and numerous lesser works on shells and insects.

There was Charles-Alexandre Lesueur, whom Maclure had met in Paris ten years before and induced to come to Philadelphia. He established himself there as a naturalist and earned his living by teaching drawing. He became a member of the Philosophical Society and a supporter of the Academy of Natural Sciences. His particular interest was ichthyology and when he came to New Harmony he began a great work on the fishes of North America, unfortunately never completed or published. He returned to France in 1837 and ended his career as Curator of the Muséum d'Histoire Naturelle at Le Havre.

One of Madame Fretageot's young ladies on board was to play a significant role in the annals of New Harmony's natural history publications. She was Lucy Sistare and was accompanied by her two sisters.

Not on the boat but also to be noted for his role in natural history publication was Cornelius Tiebout, an engraver of some reputation, who came to New Harmony with his daughter, Caroline. He was about fifty years old when he arrived in New Harmony and had recently lost a large amount of money in a business venture. The writer of the entry for him in the *Dictionary of American biography* apparently did not know that he went to New Harmony and says vaguely and misleadingly that he went to Kentucky where he died.

The program of the community at New Harmony was a mix of manual labor, recreation in the arts and intellectual activity, chiefly in the natural sciences. All property, at the beginning at least, was to be held in common and all work shared. The Boatload of Knowledge was the leavening for the intellectual life but they too were expected to work at manual tasks and Thomas Say would get blisters on his hands from digging in the garden and Madame Fretageot's pretty young students would get called away from performing on the piano to milk cows. One activity that suited them better was printing and the production of books and from 1828 onwards the press that was established there turned out an astonishing assortment of works, including some classics of American natural history.

Printing was very much in the grain of the life at New Harmony. In the spring of 1825, a year before the Boatload of Knowledge arrived, Robert Owen had bought a press at Cincinnati and installed it at New Harmony. William Wilson, in his account of New Harmony, *The angel and the serpent*, calls it a Stansbury press. I am not familiar with that name and wonder if he means Stanhope, the first of the iron presses, which were certainly available in the United States by that time. On 1 October 1825 the first number of the *New Harmony gazette* was printed on the press and thereafter it appeared every week until October 1828 when it was transferred to New York and became the *Free Enquirer*. It was the town newspaper but, as Wilson remarks, it contained very little local news beyond births, marriages, and deaths and was usually filled with the writings of Robert Owen, his son, Robert Dale Owen, Frances Wright, and William Maclure. After Maclure arrived he sought to relate the activity of printing to his own interests in education and natural sciences and to this end had another press sent up from New Orleans in 1827 for the use of the school.

The press that Maclure installed was used to print the *Disseminator*, the first issue of which came out on 16 January 1828. The full name of this journal was the *Disseminator of useful knowledge*. It was intended as a scientific journal and it did publish scientific papers such as Thomas Say's *Descriptions of new species of North American insects*, but when the *New Harmony gazette* was moved to New York in 1828, the *Disseminator* had to take on as well its function of socialistic reform and indoctrination. It was Maclure's intention to publish monographic works in natural science as well as the articles in the *Disseminator* and as early as the end of August 1827 the team of printers, engravers, and colorists necessary had been assembled. The scientists who were to conduct the research and write the monographs were already in place. A bookbinder, as the Maclure-Fretageot correspondence shows, was a continuing problem; indeed there were problems with the printers and engravers, too, over the years, but industry and patience triumphed and they produced works of distinction far superior to anything else that was being printed in Indiana at that time. The first work to be announced in the *New Harmony gazette* (29 August 1827) was Lesueur's *Fishes*—"Proposals for publishing, by subscription, a work on the Fish of North America, with Plates, drawn and colored from Nature, by C. A. Lesueur". Six weeks later came the prospectus of Thomas Say's *American conchology*. As we know the *Fishes* never appeared.* Lesueur completed only about six of the plates. *The American conchology*, however, did appear and is one of the ornaments of American natural history. Lesueur contributed two of its sixty-eight beautiful plates. The prospectus appeared in the *New Harmony gazette* for 17 and 24 October 1827:

> Proposals, for publishing by subscription, a work on the Shells of North America, with Plates, drawn and colored from Nature, by Thomas Say. This work will be published at New Harmony, Ind. under the title of American Conchology.
> It will be issued in Numbers, containing ten colored plates in each, engraved by Tiebout, together with the necessary letterpress for the description of the species presented.
> The object of this work is to fix the species of our Molluscous animals, by accurate delineation in their appropriate colors, so that they may be

---

*Josephine Elliott of New Harmony, informs me that the curator of the Muséum d'Histoire Naturelle at Le Havre reports sixteen pages of text and nine plates of Lesueur's work in the collections there.

readily recognized even by those who have not extensive cabinets for comparison.

The price to subscribers will be One Dollar each number, [increased to $1.50 on actual publication] with the right to withdraw their names on the publication of the fourth number.

The work was in fact not completed. Six parts appeared at New Harmony, a seventh at Philadelphia.

The *Conchology* did not start to appear until 1830. In the meantime another work had been announced in the *Disseminator* for 19 November 1828. This was François-André Michaux's *North American sylva*. This is the work of a man who was not associated with the New Harmony community, who had indeed left the United States to return to his native France long before the community was established. François-André Michaux and his father André had been two of the leading plant explorers in North America around the turn of the century. André wrote the first flora of eastern North America; the son wrote the first silva, the standard work until the publication of Charles Sprague Sargent's 14-volume work, *The Silva of North America*, of 1898–1902. Michaux's *Sylva* was originally published in Paris between 1810 and 1813 in French under the title *Histoire des arbres forestiers de l'Amérique septentrionale*, translated into English as the *North American sylva*, published again in Paris between 1817 and 1819 and reissued there several times. How did it come to be announced for publication at New Harmony?

The *Disseminator* prospectus explains:

Proposals for publishing Michaux's Sylva Americana [a Latin title, incidentally, which never appeared on any title page. The proposals are not signed but their author is William Maclure].

Before I left Europe, I found that a London Book-seller was on the point of purchasing the whole edition of Michaux's Sylva Americana from that author, with all the copper plates (that having only struck off about two or three hundred copies, as good as new), I interfered, and bought the whole, because I thought it a stock book that ought to be in all our libraries, as the only register of the greatest part of our forest trees,—after the cutting down of our woods will leave only the most useful in preservation,—and likewise, from the expense of publishing a new work. It is probable we shall never have another so perfect, of which the London book-seller, taking the advantage of his monopoly, would have made us pay dear for, even when the work was in the hands of the author, the London price was 10 guineas per copy.

Being in possession of all the copperplates, capable of printing thousands of copies—It is proposed to publish a new edition by subscription, in Nos. of 5 plates, coloured after nature at one dollar pr. no. It is further intended, to add a number of trees, omitted by Michaux, to make the work more complete,—and to begin the publication when one hundred subscribers shall be obtained.

Letters addressed to the editor, Michaux's Sylva Americana, New Harmony, Indiana, (post paid), with the names of those who wish to become subscribers, will be attended to—And agents will be appointed at the different places, when it will be ascertained that the number of subscribers warrant the publication.

As early as 1828 Madame Fretageot was looking for subscriptions for these works. The earliest reference we came across was in a letter from her to William Maclure dated 14 November 1828. In the transcription of the following letters I have maintained the punctuation as it appears even when it is confusing. Words in square brackets are added by me to make sense or grammar, represent guesses at illegible words or are my explanatory comments.

I have now your two letters the one from New York 24 October and from Philadelphia without date but appears [to] have been written soon after your arrival there. I am astonished you have yet no subscribers for the sylva but I hope you'll get some in both town[s] before you leave them.

Since the *Sylva* was complete in text and original copperplates it is clear that it soon became the most likely candidate for early printing and in the next letter of 12 December 1828, Mme Fretageot describes a trial run of the plates.

Mr Tiebout says it is better to have the paper sized before that the printing in colours prepares it for the brush, and otherwise one should be obliged to send it back to be sized and prepared which would cost money and time lost and not be better. ... Mr Tiebout will try this week to draw some of the trees [she means "pull some engravings of the trees"] for two purpose[s] first try the plates and 2^d to give to our boys the possibility of exercising themselves beforehand for the painting of it. I will have about 200 on our common drawing paper, it is to say 25 plates and a dozen of each to give them a fair opportunity to learn.

As twelve times twenty-five makes 300 Mme Fretageot's 200 was probably just a slip of the pen. What is of interest here is the statement that the boys of the school were going to do the hand-coloring, the sort of thing that teams of Victorian ladies in England and elsewhere did for so many plate books of the time.

In a letter of 2 January 1829, Mme Fretageot reports that the trial run had been carried out. "Our schollars" she says, "... really do it very well. This is as much for their improvement and to prepare them for the work as well as for the trying of the plates which succeeds quite well 12 of each will amount 1872 [there were 156 plates all together] the greatest part of them will serve for the first numbers when it will be published." A letter in November of that year says, "We have not received yet the paper for the Sylva" and there is some complaint about Tiebout's slowness in pulling engravings, which continues to be echoed in later correspondence.

During the course of the next year, for reasons that are not very clear, work on the *Sylva* was abandoned in favor of Say's *American conchology*. Perhaps there were not enough subscriptions—there were copies of the Paris edition in English available besides those that Maclure had bought. On 22 November 1830, Mme Fretageot writes to Maclure, "The first number of Say's work on shells is now in hand and it will appear in the middle of next month". The first number did in fact appear before the end of the year in buff wrappers, with a dedication "To William Maclure, President of the Academy of Natural Sciences of Philadelphia and of the American Geological Society; Member of the American Philosophical Society, &c.&c. this book is dedicated as a small but sincere tribute of respect and friendship, by his much obliged friend The Author". There were ten engravings by Cornelius Tiebout, made from drawings by Mrs Say. Who was Mrs Say? She was Lucy Sistare, one of Mme Fretageot's charges already mentioned and, according to the Duke of Saxe-Weimar, who visited New Harmony in 1826, "the handsomest and most polished of the female world" there. Thomas Say thought so too and put aside his work on shells and insects to engage in a romantic elopement. A letter written by W. C. Pelham, an accountant in the New Harmony store, to his father, dated 10 January 1827, recounts the story:

> Say was married to Lucy Sistare the other day. They ran off by themselves to a place beyond Springfield and were married by a Squire's somebody who doubtless thought the party a queer set from the account they gave of it. On coming back, the carriage overset and Virginia [Virginia Du Palais, who had gone along as a bridesmaid] hurt her face very much and Louisa [Louisa Neef] her shoulder, but both are now well.

Madame Fretageot appears to have forgiven Lucy and Thomas and took them both under her wing. Lucy became a good artist, a patient colorist and, inevitably, a student of conchology. Later she was to be the first woman elected to the Academy of Natural Sciences.

On 24 February 1831, Tiebout's daughter, Caroline, was married to the young man who was then doing the hand printing. Mme Fretageot writes:

> Our hand printer Kellogg will be married the 24 of this month to Caroline Tiebout. It is a match well calculated and it pleases me that girl makes a good marriage Kellogg is a nice young man actif industrous and much willing to follow my advice on economy. Caroline will also work at colouring the Conchology and can make 2 dollars per week, it will attach both to the establishment and be both useful.

By April she did not think so highly of Kellogg, who had formed his own ideas of economy.

> That young man has obliged me to raise his wages to 24 dollars a month, and if I am not mistaken he has driven away Lyman Lyon and James Bennett [who had been working at the printing office] in order to secure a place which he would be sorry to loose. Which raises my suspicion is that he was always talking about prices a printer gets at Louisville or Cincinnati, those two young fools have listened to it and Lyman who I expected would have been able to conduct the office has left the School and is now learning engraving with Tiebout in spite of what I could say to the old man. Say think[s] that it will be no difficulty to engage an engraver to come here who will do four times as much work as he [i.e. Tiebout] does.

The second number of the *Conchology* was published in April of that year (1831) with the imprint, "Printed at the School Press", used for the first time, and in September the third number came out with an error in the year, which was given as 1830.

On 4 November of the same year Mme Fretageot left New Harmony to spend a year in Paris, where, surprisingly enough, she still had a husband. Thomas Say was now left in charge of the printing house and we trace the progress of the *Conchology* in his letters to Mme Fretageot to whom he chose to write rather than to Maclure. In a letter of 5 January 1832, he writes to her: "We have not yet got out the 4th No. of the Conchology;" to which he adds modestly, "the subscribers at least some of them appear to be satisfied with it". On 29 February 1832, he writes:

We are dashing on with the printing office at a great rate, with plenty of ink and paper and force. Mr Tiebout is extremely ill and I have but little hope of his recovery. Lyman [i.e. Lyman Lyon whose learning engraving from Tiebout Mme Fretageot had deprecated] improves rapidly in his engraving & has executed several plates himself.

In a postscript to a letter of 30 July 1832 Say writes:

She [i.e. Lucy] has coloured five thousand plates of the Conchology since you left us, which is more than double the number she ever did before in the same time. [That works out to about 19 plates a day. What happened to all the little boys? If she did the entire coloring for the 4th and 5th parts that would indicate a subscription list of about 250. Considering how few copies of this work exist today I think it was probably nearer half of that]. The 4th No. was published in March. The 5th is coloured already & ready to send, and only waits the covers which I hope are at Mt. Vernon, & if so it can be published within a week.

The back cover of the fourth number contained an announcement of Tiebout's death.

Since the publication of the preceding No. we have had to regret the decease of Mr Tiebout, engraver for this work, but it is hoped that this bereavement will not much retard the publication of the work in future.

I suspect Say thought it would go much faster now that poor old Tiebout was out of the picture.

Five of the plates in the fourth number were engraved by Lyman Lyon. By the fifth number he had taken over all the engraving. Say writes on 28 August.

Lyman Lyon engraves now tolerably well, he does all the engraving for the conchology and can work as rapidly as Lucy can colour. ... We have sent off the 5th No. of the Conchology to the subscribers, & the engravings and the colouring for the 6th is in rapid execution. ... Mr Tiebout's engraving tools &c. have been sold by his executors and we bought them for the establishment as we could not do without them.

On 1 October he writes:

Lucy is now colouring the 6th no. of the Conchology which will be published as soon as possible. I wish I could be with you in Paris for a few days, to furnish myself with an assortment of useful *colors* and *brushes*

and to improve myself in the art of coloring—I must resign and go to the
kitchen to make up some bread which cannot be so easily dispensed with
as the paints and brushes—The Conchology seems to be approved of by
the critics & its patronage is extending.

The sixth number was not published until April 1834 and its tardiness is
explained by a note on the back of the wrapper.

The long delay in the publication of this number has been occasioned by
the protracted illness and final decease of our engraver Mr Lyon. A young
man of amiable manners and much promise in his profession.

By that date, in fact a year earlier, Mme Fretageot herself had died. After
leaving Paris she had sailed to visit Maclure in Mexico, expressing the hope
of seeing him "as soon as possible". Her hope appears to have been barely
fulfilled since she died in Mexico City. As Arthur Bestor remarks, in his
Education and reform at New Harmony, "New Harmony was Madame
Fretageot's monument as truly as it was Rapp's or Owen's or Maclure's.
The wise management she had given at the outset enabled Maclure's threefold
enterprise to function effectively throughout the succeeding decade, and to
spread its influence beyond". It is not possible for anyone who knows the
story of New Harmony to walk the streets of that place today without
thinking of Marie Louise Duclos Fretageot, that indomitable woman who
played no small part in its history. She had begun the work on Michaux's
Sylva but for some years now nothing more had been heard of it. Then
suddenly out of the blue on 16 November 1833 appears a letter from William
Maclure to Thomas Say.

Publish the silva in any way you like only remember that cheapness is the
end and sole object of our [enterprise].

This needs a comment. Maclure was concerned with cheapness for one
reason only. He did not want to skimp on such things as the quality of the
paper or the printing or the handcoloring of illustrations but he did want
the work to be available at a reasonable and economical price to the common
man. Long before Thomas Huxley's lectures to Working Men's Clubs in
England, Maclure was concerned for advancing the education of those who
did not have money or opportunity. Did Say plan to bring out the *Sylva*?
We found no evidence of it. Some considerable amount of work had been
done on the plates at least in Mme Fretageot's time but I do not know if
any of the printing of the text had been done. Less than a year after Maclure's
letter, in any event, Thomas Say himself was dead of typhus fever and
dysentery. He drove himself hard, "dashing on", as he might have said,
with his work and the work of the community from which he had hoped to
be relieved by Mme Fretageot's return. He went for long periods of time
without food or sleep and, under these pressures, his normally robust
constitution succumbed to the prevailing diseases of the place and time.

Maclure's brother, Alexander, wrote from New Harmony on 14 October
1834 to William, four days after Say's death.

The work on the conchology of course stops but as part was finished all
but the Manuscript which no one here can finish. It was Mr Say's desire

that it should be put into the hands of Mr Dobson of Philadelphia who may probably be able to do something with it.

A seventh part was in fact published about four years later in 1838 (the date is not certain), printed in Philadelphia. Its eight plates were drawn by Lucy Say. There was some talk of continuing it with the help of T. A. Conrad, who had worked on the seventh part, but it came to nothing.

Besides the *Conchology* Say had eleven other works, mostly small pamphlets, printed at New Harmony. Most of them are quite rare.

What of Michaux's *Sylva*? It was finally printed in 1841, a year after Maclure himself had died in Mexico. The imprint on the title page shows it was published at Philadelphia by J. Dobson, 106 Chestnut Street, but printed by William Amphlett, New Harmony, Indiana.

Amphlett was born in England and came to the United States in 1818 where he bought a farm in Springfield, Ohio. He went to New Harmony in 1836, attracted by the promise of education. He was given the job of proof correcting at the press by Alexander, William Maclure's brother. Two years later he became editor of the *Disseminator* and eventually proprietor of that journal. He it was then who finally brought out the *Sylva* in three volumes thirteen years after Mme Fretageot had started to look for subscribers, and a beautiful job he made of it. A year later it was reissued in Cincinnati and Amphlett's name appears there as publisher along with Doolittle and Munson. Did he then move to Cincinnati? We do not know though we do know that he cared for the New Harmony climate as little as Maclure himself had done since he wrote in a letter to him in 1839.

I do not like the atmosphere of the Wabash valley. The transitions from the extremes of aridity to a saturating humidity are too common.

The physical climate may leave something to be desired. The intellectual climate, however, of the little village on the Wabash, engendered by the men and women of the Boatload of Knowledge, was such as to flourish for half a century and draw to it scholars and visitors from Europe and elsewhere. It still does. Though Owen and Maclure and Say and Lesueur and Marie-Louise Fretageot are long gone the visitor to New Harmony today, walking the quiet streets under the Golden Rain Trees (which Thomas Say planted) will find it imbued with their spirit. Utopia may not have been established here but it was a brave attempt and if nothing else, *litera scripta manet*—the written word remains in the rich treasury of letters written by the participants, preserved in the vault of Maclure's Workingmen's Institute. *Litera impressa manet*, the printed word remains in the constellation of publications that issued from New Harmony, of which Say's *American conchology* and Michaux's *North American sylva* are the brightest stars.

A BIBLIOGRAPHY OF THE WORKS BY THOMAS SAY AND FRANÇOIS-ANDRÉ
MICHAUX
PRINTED AT NEW HARMONY, INDIANA

This bibliography contains only monographic works. Say contributed frequently to *The Disseminator* but his contributions are not noted here though there are some references to them in the *Notes*. Under *References* I have noted only those libraries in which I have actually examined copies.

Say, Thomas (1787-1834)

1. *Descriptions of some new terrestrial and fluviatile shells of North America.*
[New Harmony, the school press, 1829]
No title page.

Collation: 8°: 9ℓ., unsigned, unpaginated

Contents: On ℓ. *1*r drop title, "Descriptions of some new Terrestrial and Fluviatile Shells of North America. By Thomas Say."; ℓ. *1-9* text.

References: Byrd and Peckham 391; Lilly Library (Indiana University).

Notes: This is an offprint of descriptions first printed in *The Disseminator of useful knowledge*, a New Harmony journal. They appeared in the issues of 29 July, 12, 26 August, 9, 23 September, 7, 21 October, and 4, 18 November 1829. According to Byrd and Peckham the type was held after each issue, some rules, the running heads and page numbers were removed, the type rearranged without any resetting and copies were run off. The work is printed in two columns, beginning with *Helix lucubrata* and ending with *Cyclas triangularis*.

   Above the drop title in the Lilly copy there is an ink inscription, "Recd this from Mrs. Say" and, below the drop title, "July 29-1829". That is the date of the first appearance of these descriptions in *The Disseminator*.

   Under *Unio ridibundus* there is a reference to *flagellatus* Nob. (see *American conchology*).

2. *Descriptions of new species of North American insects.* New Harmony, 1829-1833.

   Descriptions of new species of North American insects, and observations on some of the species already described. By Thomas Say. New Harmony, Indiana. 1829-1833.

Collation: 8°: 38ℓ., unsigned; [ii] *1-17* [1] 18-65 46-53 (corrected in pencil in Lilly copy to "66-73").

Contents: ℓ.*1* title, v□; ℓ. *2-3* text in small type, double columns; ℓ. *4-9* text in small type, single column; ℓ. *9*v□; ℓ.*10-38* text in large type, single column, dated at foot of ℓ. *10*, "August 20, 1830."

References: Byrd and Peckham 390, Lilly Library (Indiana University).

Notes: Byrd and Peckham declare the Lilly Library copy incomplete. A complete copy (Harvard University Library) should have a page numbered $73\frac{1}{2}$ (recto), followed by 74 through 80, (i.e. 4 more leaves in all). The first 17 pages are offprinted from *The Disseminator* as follows, *fide* Byrd and Peckham:

1-2	Vol. 3 no. 5, 17 March, 1830
3-4	Vol. 3 no. 15, 12 May, 1830
5-6	n.s. Vol. 1, no. 1, 29 June, 1830
7-9	n.s. Vol. 1, no. 3, 13 July, 1830
9-11	n.s. Vol. 1, no. 4, 20 July, 1830
11-13	n.s. Vol. 1, no. 5, 27 July, 1830
13-15	n.s. Vol. 1, no. 6, 3 August, 1830
15-17	n.s. Vol. 1, no. 7, 10 August, 1830

The work appears to have been published in blue wrappers but these are lacking in the Lilly copy, which has "Gift of Mrs. Say" inscribed in pencil on the title page.

3. *American conchology, or descriptions of the shells of North America.* New Harmony, 1830 [-1838?].

American conchology, or Descriptions of the Shells of North America. Illustrated by coloured figures from original drawings executed from nature: By Thomas Say, F.M.L.S. Member of many learned Societies in Europe and America. "Read Nature; Nature is a friend to Truth." Young. New Harmony, Indiana. Printed at the School Press, 1830.

Collation: see *Notes.*

Contents: see *Notes.*

Plates: 68 engravings, numbered 1-68 except 65, unnumbered; all from drawings by Lucy Say, signed "Mrs. Say Del.", except 51, 52, by Charles-Alexandre Lesueur, signed "C.A. Lesueur del.", engraved by Cornelius Tiebout (1-30, 33-34, 36), Lyman Lyon (32, 35, 38-50, 51-53, 55), I. Walker (54, 56-60, 61, 63, 66, 68) and unsigned (31, 37, 62, 64, 65, 67); all hand colored.

References: Byrd and Peckham 414,415, 449, 450, 485, 486, 557, Walker 93; Workingmen's Institute Library (New Harmony), Lilly Library (Indiana University), Purdue University Library, Regenstein Library (University of Chicago), State Library of Ohio (Columbus, Ohio).

Notes: the *American conchology* was published in six parts at New Harmony with a seventh part appearing, after Say's death, at Philadelphia. Of the half-dozen copies I have seen no two are the same and the work needs further detailed investigation. The bibliographic details of the seven parts are noted below.

1. [Buff wrappers] Vol. I. No. I. Price $1,50, coloured. 1830.

Collation: 8°: A^4 B-E^4; unpaginated, 20ℓ.

Contents: A_1 title, v☐; A_2 dedication "To William Maclure, President of the Academy of Natural Sciences of Philadelphia, and of the American Geological Society; Member of the American Philosophical Society, &c. &c. this book is dedicated as a small, but sincere tribute of respect and friendship, by his much obliged friend The Author.", v☐; A_3-E_4 text.

Plates: 1-10

Notes: There are two issues of this part. An erratum on the back wrapper reads "In the Observations on *Unio Ridibundus*, for "flagellatus, Nob." read *sulcatus*, Lea."

The Workingmen's Institute Library copy and the Lilly Library copy both have the first uncorrected issue; whereas Purdue University Library has the second corrected issue. Bernard Quaritch recently offered both issues in their catalogue 1014 of 1981.

2. [Buff wrappers] Vol. I. No. II. April 1831. Printed at the School Press.

Collation: 8°: F–I^4 J^4; unpaginated, 20ℓ.

Contents: F$_1$–J$_{3r}$ text; J$_{3v}$□; J$_4$□.

Plates: 11–20.

Notes: The collation of signatures is unusual in using both I and J. J4 is sometimes omitted since it is a blank leaf. It is present in the Lilly Library copy.

3. [Buff wrappers] No. III. September 1831 [wrapper bears erroneous date "1830"]. Printed at the School Press.

Collation: 8°: K–O^4; unpaged, 20ℓ.

Contents: K$_1$–O$_{4r}$ text: O$_4$v□.

Plates: 21–30.

4. [Buff wrappers] No. IV. March 1832.

Collation: 8°: P–S^4 T^2; unsigned, unpaginated, 18ℓ.

Contents: P$_1$–T$_2$ text.

Plates: 31–40.

Notes: The back wrapper contains the announcement of Tiebout's decease.

5. [Buff wrappers] No. V. August 1832. Printed at the M Press.

Collation: 8°: V–Z^4 2A^4; unpaginated, 20ℓ.

Contents: V$_1$–2A$_4$ text.

Plates: 41–50.

Notes: The back wrapper contains the following notice: "With this Number we send gratis to those who have paid for the preceding Nos., a copy of a work which we have recently printed, entitled "Glossary to the American Conchology," [see no. 10] explanatory of the terms made use of in the science of Conchology."

6. [Buff wrappers] No. VI. April 1834. Printed at the M Press.

Collation: 8°: 2B–2D^4 2E^1 2F–2G^4; unpaginated, 21ℓ.

Contents: 2B$_1$–2G$_3$ text;2G$_4$rv An attempt to exhibit a synonymy of the Western, North American species of the genera Unio and Alasmodonta.

Plates: 51–60.

Notes: The back wrapper contains the announcement of Lyman Lyon's decease. Six months later Thomas Say himself was dead and no further parts were printed at New Harmony.

7. [Blue wrappers] No. VII. [erroneously as "VIII" in some copies] n.p. n.d. [Philadelphia, 1838?].

Collation: 8°: 1^4 2^4 3^1; unpaginated, 9ℓ.

Contents: 1$_1$–2$_4$ text; 3$_1$r□; 3$_1$v appendix.

Plates: 61–68.

Notes: There are two issues of this part. The University of Chicago Regenstein Library copy collates $1-2^4$ 3^2 and the appendix is on 3_2rv. T. A. Conrad was responsible for preparing this part from Say's manuscript. The eight plates are by Mrs Say.

Some copies that I have examined (Workingmen's Institute Library and Regenstein Library) have no signed gatherings after O, that is in parts 4-6.

4. *New terrestrial and fluviatile shells of North America.* [New Harmony] 1831.

No title page.

Collation: 8°: 3ℓ., unsigned, unpaginated.

Contents: On ℓ. *1*r drop title, "New terrestrial and fluviatile Shells of North America. By Thomas Say", followed by the words, "The following observations and descriptions have been made since the publication of my last essay." ℓ. *1-3*r text; ℓ. *3*v☐.

References: Byrd and Peckham 455, Lilly Library (Indiana University).

Notes: This is another off-print of material first published in *The Disseminator*. It first appeared in the issues of 30 December, 1830, and 29 January, 1831. At the bottom of the first page is printed the date, "January 1st, 1831".

5. *Descriptions of new species of North American insects.* New Harmony 1831.

   Descriptions of new species of North American insects, found in Louisiana by Joseph Barabino. By Thomas Say. March 1831. Indiana. Printed at the School Press, New-Harmony.

Collation: 8°: 1^4 2^4 3^2; *1-3* 4-19 [1].

Contents: 1_1 title, v☐; 1_2-3_2r text; 3_2v☐.

References: Byrd and Peckham 454, Walker 108.

Notes: I have seen no original copy of this work and my description is made from a photocopy of the Boston Society of Natural History copy provided by the Academy of Natural Sciences in Philadelphia.

6. *Descriptions of new species of curculionites of North America.* New Harmony, Indiana, 1831.

   Descriptions of new species of Curculionites of North America, with observations on some of the species already known. By Thomas Say. New Harmony, Indiana. July 1831.

Collation: 8°: π^1 1^4 $2-3^4$ $4^{4;}$ [ii] *1* 2-30 [2].

Contents: π1 title, v☐; 1_1-1_4 text in large type; 2_1-3_4 text in small type; 4_1-4_3 supplement in large type; 4_4rv☐.

References: Byrd and Peckham 451, Walker 106; Lilly Library (Indiana University).

Notes: The title-page of the Lilly copy is inscribed in pencil "from Mrs Say to J. E. McKay".

7. *Descriptions of new species of heteropterous Hemiptera of North America.*
New Harmony, 1831.

Descriptions of new species of heteropterous Hemiptera of North America.
By Thomas Say. New-Harmony, Indiana. Dec. 1831.

Collation: 8°: A^4 B-E^4; *1* 2-39 [1].

Contents: *A*1r title; *A*1v-E4r text; E4v□.

References: Byrd and Peckham 452 (31p. only), Lilly Library (Indiana University).

Notes: In the Lilly copy someone has pencilled in beside the printed pagination the numerals 32 to 69.

8. *Descriptions of new species of heteropterous Hemiptera of North America.*
New Harmony, 1831. 69 p.

References: Byrd and Peckham 453, Walker 107.

Notes: I have seen no copy of this work and think it may be a ghost. None of the three libraries cited by the *National Union Catalogue* as having it were able to produce it. The question needs further investigation.

9. *New species of North American insects.* New Harmony, 1832.

New species of North American insects, found by Joseph Barabino, chiefly in Louisiana. By Thomas Say. January, 1832. Indiana, printed at the School Press, New-Harmony.

Collation: 8°: 1^4 2^4; *1-3* 4-16.

Contents: 1_1 title, v□; 1_2-2_4 text.

References: Byrd and Peckham 488.

Notes: Not seen. My description is made from a photocopy in the Indiana Historical Society Library, Indianapolis. The only location of this rarest of Say's New Harmony publications is given by Byrd and Peckham as the Boston Medical Library. That library was transferred in 1956 to the Francis A. Countway Library of Medicine, Harvard Medical Library, and since the move of the huge collection, the Say pamphlet has not come to light.

10. *A glossary to Say's Conchology.* New Harmony 1832.

A glossary to Say's Conchology. New Harmony, Indiana. Printed by Richard Beck & James Bennett. 1832.

Collation: 8°: π^2 1^2 2-6^2 7^2; [iv] *1* 2-25 [3]

Contents: π1 title, v□; π2rv□; 1_1-6_2v explanation of terms used in conchology; on 6_2v-7_1r general rules relative to diminutive compounds. [From Kirby and Spence.]; on 7_1r Rule for the pronunciation of the Linnaean names. [From Withering.] 7_1v-7_2□.

References: Byrd and Peckham 487, Walker 123; Lilly Library (Indiana University).

Notes: See *Notes* to no. 3:5.

11. *Catalogue of exotic shells in my cabinet 1833* [n.p.n.d.]

No title page. The work appears to have been bound in blue wrappers but these are now lacking in the Lilly copy. The title may have been printed on the front wrapper.

Collation: 8°: A–D^4 E^1; 1–33 [1]

Contents: On A$_1$r, drop title, "Catalogue of exotic Shells in my cabinet 1833."; A$_1$–D$_4$ main text; E$_1$ [addendum] "CEPHALOPODES in my collection, 1833."

References: Lilly Library (Indiana University).

Notes: Under the drop title on the first page of the Lilly copy is the ink inscription "T. Say". Someone has pencilled in beside the pagination on all rectos the numerals 144 to 176. There is no indication that the work was printed at New Harmony but the type appears to be the same as that used for *Descriptions of some new terrestrial and fluviatile shells* [New Harmony, the School Press, 1829]. Attached to the Lilly copy are three leaves of manuscript titled "Index to Says paper". The index begins with "Abax 88" and ends with "Zygops 80" and is apparently unrelated to this work.

12. *Descriptions of some new terrestrial and fluviatile shells of North America.* 1829, 1830, 1831. New Harmony, 1840.

Descriptions of some new terrestrial and fluviatile shells of North America. 1829, 1830, 1831. By Thomas Say, F.M.L.S., &c. New Harmony, Indiana. 1840.

Collation: 8°: *1*^{4} 2–3^4 4^1; *1–5* 6–26

Contents: *1*$_1$ title, v☐; *1*$_2$[preface] signed "Lucy W. Say April, 1840."; *1*$_3$–4$_1$ text.

References: Walker 288; Lilly Library (Indiana University).

Notes: The work is published in buff wrappers. Lucy Say's prefatory material is worth quoting in its entirety as an explanation for this publication. She says:

The following descriptions of some new Terrestrial and Fluviatile Shells of North America, were originally published in the Transylvania Journal, also in the Disseminator, a weekly periodical published at New Harmony, Indiana, prior to the publication of the American Conchology, into which they were to have been copied with illustrative Drawings. This object having only been partially accomplished, it seems necessary for their preservation and more general circulation, to have them republished in a more collective form.

The following will be found a complete list of such as were omitted in that work.

I regret exceedingly my inability to accompany the figured species with drawings.

If any specimens of species here described are not contained in the Cabinet of the Academy of Natural Sciences, they will most probably be found in my own private collection, which has not been opened since it was put up five years since. If this should be the case, it will afford me much pleasure to place them in that collection for future reference.

13. Michaux, François-André (1770–1855). *The North American sylva.*
Philadelphia 1841. 8°. 3 vols.

The North American sylva; or, a description of the forest trees of the
United States, Canada, and Nova Scotia, considered particularly with
respect to their use in the arts, and their introduction into commerce; to
which is added a description of the most useful of the European forest
trees. Illustrated by 156 coloured engravings. Translated from the French
of F. Andrew Michaux, Member of the American Philosophical Society
of Philadelphia; Correspondent of the Institute of France; Member of
the Agricultural Societies of Charleston, S.C., Philadelphia and Massachusetts; Honorary Member of the Historical, Literary and Philosophical
Societies of New York... arbore sulcamus maria, terrasque admovemus,
arbore exædificamus tecta. Plinii Secundi Nat. Hist., lib. xii. With three
additional volumes, containing all the Forest Trees discovered in the
Rocky Mountains, the Territory of Oregon, down to the shores of the
Pacific and into the confines of California, as well as in various parts
of the United States. Illustrated by122 finely coloured plates. By Thomas
Nuttall, F.L.S., Member of the American Philosophical Society, and of
the Academy of Natural Sciences of Philadelphia, &c. &c. &c. The whole
forming six volumes, and comprising 278 plates. Vol. I. Containing
Plates from 1 to 50. [Vol. II. Containing Plates from 51 to 100.] [Vol.
III. Containing Plates from 101 to 156.] Philadelphia: J. Dobson, 106
Chestnut Street. Printed by William Amphlett, New Harmony, Indiana.
1841.

Collation: 8°: [vol. 1] $\pi 1^4$ $\pi 2^4$ $\pi 3^1$ 1–15^4 16^1; *i–v* vi *vii–ix* x–xi *xii–xiii* xiv–xviii
1 2–122. [vol. 2] π^2 16^3 17–23^4 1–9^4 10^1; [iv] 123–184 1–74. [vol. 3] π^2 10^3
11–27^4; [iv] 75 76–216.

Contents: [vol. 1] $\pi 1_1$, title, v copyright notice; $\pi 1_2$ dedication, v□; $\pi 1_3$
contents; $\pi 1_4$ list of plates in vol. 1, v□; $\pi 2_1$–$\pi 2_2$r preface, signed "A.L.H.,
Paris, May 20, 1819." $\pi 2_{2v}$; $\pi 2_3$–$\pi 3_1$ introduction; 1_1–1_2r oaks; 1_{2v}–1_3r methodical disposition of the oaks; 1_{3v}–7_2 text; 7_3–7_4 additions to the oaks; 8_1 walnuts;
8_2r methodical disposition of the walnuts; 8_{2v}–11$_4$ text; 12$_1$–12$_2$ recapitulation
of the property and the uses of hickory wood; 12$_3$r maples; 12$_{3v}$ methodical
disposition of the maples; 12$_4$–16$_1$ text. [vol. 2] $\pi 1$ title, v copyright notice;
$\pi 2$ contents of vol. 2; 16$_2$r magnolias; 16$_{2v}$–21$_3$r text; 21$_{3v}$□; 21$_4$r birches; 21$_{4v}$
methodical disposition of the birches; 22$_1$–23$_1$ text; 1$_1$–10$_1$ text. [vol. 3] $\pi 1$
title, v copyright notice (1842); $\pi 2$ contents of vol. 3; 10$_2$–14$_1$r text; 14$_{1v}$
ashes; 14$_2$–17$_3$ text; 17$_4$r pines; 17$_{4v}$ methodical disposition of the pines and
spruces; 18$_1$–23$_1$r text; 23$_{1v}$ cypresses; 24$_1$–25$_2$ text; 25$_3$–27$_4$ recapitulation of
the uses of North American trees.

Plates: 156 stipple engravings, color-printed, retouched by hand, number
[vol. 1] 1–50, [vol. 2] 51–100, [vol. 3] 101–156; of leaves, flowers and fruits
of trees, from drawings by Bessa (92), P. J. Redouté (32), H. J. Redouté
(27), A. Riché (3), A. Redouté (1), and 1 unsigned, engraved by various
hands, title with English name and Latin binomial.

References: Byrd and Peckham 942, Walker 315, MacPhail, *Michaux* 21a;
Lilly Library (Indiana University), Gray Herbarium/Arnold Arboretum

Libraries, Missouri Botanical Garden Library, New York Botanical Garden Library, American Philosophical Society.

Notes: This is the first edition of Michaux's work to be printed in the United States. As the title-page indicates it was intended to add three supplemntary volumes by Thomas Nuttall but these were not printed by Amphlett. They were not published until 1842–1849. Only the first volume was published by J. Dobson, who was also the publisher of the present work, and it has a quite distinct title-page. Each of the other volumes was put out by a different publisher.

It seems odd for Amphlett to have included a mention of Nuttall's volumes on his title-pages but he may have been persuaded to do so by Dobson in the belief that these supplementary volumes would be ready much sooner than they in fact were.

This edition was reissued at Cincinnati in the following year, without mention of Nuttall's supplement on the title-page.

ACKNOWLEDGEMENTS

I thank Josephine Elliott, New Harmony, Indiana, for much help and advice; Aline Cook, Librarian, Workingmen's Institute, New Harmony, for making available original manuscripts and printed works in the Institute's collections and for permission to quote from them; and Ralph G. Schwarz, President, Historic New Harmny, Inc., for assistance and advice. These three persons also read my paper in an early version, corrected some errors of fact and made useful suggestions, for which I am grateful.

I also thank Marjorie S. Dickinson, Librarian, Kingwood Center, Mansfield, Ohio, who transcribed many of the letters; Betsy Levins, The Morton Arboretum, who typed and retyped the manuscript several times for this final printed version; and the many librarians who made available works in their collections or provided photocopies and information, in particular, Sylva Baker and Janet Evans, Academy of Natural Sciences, Philadelphia, William R. Cagle, Lilly Library, Indiana University, Bloomington, Indiana, and Keith Dowden, Purdue University Libraries, West Lafayette, Indiana.

Finally, I thank Dr Emanuel D. Rudolph, Department of Botany, Ohio State University, Columbus, who encouraged me to pursue the subject of New Harmony printings of natural history works.

REFERENCES

BANTA, R. E., *The American concology: a venture in backwoods book printing.* In *The Colophon*, N.S. **3**(1): 24–40.

BESTOR, Arthur E. 1948 *Education and reform at New Harmony: correspondence of William Maclure and Marie Duclos Fretageot, 1820–1833*. Indianapolis, Indiana Historical Society. Reprinted Clifton, New Jersey, Augustus M. Kelley, 1973.

BYRD, Cecil K. and PECKHAM, Howard H., 1955 *A bibliography of Indiana imprints 1804–1853*. Indianapolis, Indiana Historical Bureau.

ELLIOTT, Josephine M. ed. 1969 *To Holland and to New Harmony:Robert Dale Owen's travel journal, 1825–1826*. Indianapolis Indiana Historical Society.

LOCKWOOD, George B., 1905 *The New Harmony movement*. New York, Appleton. Reprinted New York, Dover, 1971.

MACPHAIL, Ian, 1981 *André and François-André Michaux* (Sterling Morton Library bibliographies in botany and horticulture, I.) [Lisle, Illinois] The Morton Arboretum.

PEATTIE, Donald Culross, 1936 *Green laurels*. New York, Simon and Schuster.

WALKER, Mary Alden, 1934 *The beginnings of printing in the state of Indiana*. Crawfordsville, Indiana, R. E. Banta.

WILSON, William E., 1964 *The angel and the serpent: the story of New Harmony*. Bloomington, Indiana University Press.

WILLIAM BARTRAM AND HIS TRAVELS

Robert McCracken Peck
Special Assistant to the President
The Academy of Natural Sciences,
19th and the Parkway, Philadelphia,
Pennsylvania 19103

In the spring of 1773, American naturalist William Bartram left his home near Philadelphia on a lone journey of exploration that would carry him 2,400 miles through North and South Carolina, Georgia, East and West Florida and the uncharted Indian territories to the west. The trip took Bartram four years to complete and resulted in one of the great American literary works of the eighteenth century.

Bartram's stated objective in undertaking the ambitious trip was to discover on behalf of his English patron John Fothergill, "rare and useful productions of nature, chiefly in the vegetable kingdom". To Bartram the publication of *Travels* was only an outgrowth of a scientific quest.

Ironically, the effect of the book on European readers was such that Bartram's reputation as a writer soon overshadowed his many scientific accomplishments. Because most of the subsequent European editions of *Travels* were "pirated" or published without his knowledge, permission or renumeration, it is quite likely that he never fully realized the popularity or impact of his book. He certainly never benefited from it.

William inherited his interest in natural history from his father, John Bartram (1699–1777) who, for almost half a century, was recognized as America's foremost botanist. From the time of his early childhood, William accompanied his father on collecting trips in and around Philadelphia and as far north as the Catskills in New York. The plants they gathered in the wild were carefully propagated in the Bartrams' botanical garden and from there distributed to various parts of the world.

Although largely self-educated and a man of modest means, John Bartram counted among his friends and correspondents many of the leading intellectuals on both sides of the Atlantic: Benjamin Franklin, James Logan, Cadwallader Colden, Joseph Brientnall, and William Byrd—all recognized the older Bartram's many remarkable talents and embraced him as a friend. Johann Dillenius, Philip Miller, Peter Collinson and other English naturalists exchanged seeds, specimens, and ideas with the ingenious American, whom they knew only by reputation and correspondence. Swedish taxonomist Carl Linnaeus once described John Bartram as "the greatest natural botanist in the world".

Raised in this stimulating intellectual environment, William Bartram quickly developed an inherent curiosity about, and respect for, natural science. Unlike

Contributions to the History of North American Natural History. Society for the Bibliography of Natural History, London, 1983.

his father, William benefited from a rigorous period of formal education at
the Philadelphia Academy, where he studied history, Latin, French, and the
classics.

Throughout his childhood William demonstrated an unusual native talent
in art. His paintings of birds and flowers were so accomplished that John
Bartram soon took to sending them, along with his own letters and collected
seeds, to Peter Collinson, a wealthy London cloth merchant and naturalist
who had sponsored many of the older Bartram's collecting trips. Collinson
was sufficiently impressed with the quality of William's work to share the
paintings with a number of other influential collectors in London. They, in
turn, sent orders to William for paintings of birds, plants, shells, and other
"natural curiosities". One of these patrons was John Fothergill, a London
physician who later supported the four-year expedition described in Bartram's
Travels.

William Bartram did not receive his father's undivided attention during
the formative years of his life—he was the seventh of eleven children—but
in many ways he was the closest to his father and probably spent more time
with him than any of the other children. He could not have had a better
instructor.

John's letters reflect his great pride in William's accomplishments. They
also suggest some paternal concern. In a 1755 letter to Peter Collinson, John
wrote:

> My son William is just turned sixteen. It is now time to propose some way
> for him to get his living by. I don't want him to be what is commonly
> called a gentleman. I want to put him to some business by which he may,
> with care and industry, get a temperate, reasonable living. I am afraid that
> botany and drawing will not afford him one, and hard labour don't agree
> with him. I have designed, several years, to put him to a doctor, to learn
> physic and surgery; but that will take him from his drawing, which he
> takes particular delight in.

Despite repeated efforts by the elder Bartram and his friends to launch
William on a business career, the young man continued to focus his attention
on plants, birds and drawing.

In 1761, at the age of 21, William gave up a frustrating business appren-
ticeship in Philadelphia and for the first time struck off on his own. He
traveled to North Carolina to live with the family of his father's half-brother,
William, who owned a trading post at Cape Fear. Although his business
acumen did not improve with the change of latitude ("everything goes wrong
with him there" observed John), the independence Bartram achieved through
his stay in the South seemed to give him new self confidence.

In 1765, through the intercession of Peter Collinson and others, John
Bartram received an appointment as botanist to King George III which
provided both prestige and renumeration in the form of a fifty pound annual
stipend. He invited William to accompany him on a year-long collecting trip
through North and South Carolina, Georgia, and Florida. Florida, which
had come under British control in 1763, was the primary object of the

William Bartram (1739–1823) by Charles Willson Peale.
(Reproduced from the collection of Independence National Historical Park
Collection, Philadelphia.)

expedition and a place both Bartrams had desired to visit for some time. (Considerably larger than the present state, Florida then extended as far west as the Mississippi and to the 31st parallel on the north.)

The trip proved extremely successful and helped to enhance the reputations of both father and son within scientific circles in Europe. For William, the expedition opened rich new collecting areas and intimations that patronage could be obtained from abroad for exploration, collection and scientific study.

When his father returned to Philadelphia in 1766 William decided to remain in Florida in an attempt to start an indigo plantation near St Augustine. But this, like his other business ventures, proved unsuccessful.

Henry Laurens, a South Carolinian who later served as President of the Continental Congress, wrote to John Bartram in August 1766 with a description of William's condition. "No colouring can do justice to the forlorn state of poor Billy Bartram," he reported:

A gentle, mild young man, no wife, no friend, no companion, no neighbor, no human inhabitant within nine miles of him, the nearest by water, no boat to come at them, and these only common soliders... seated upon a beggarly spot of land, scant of the bare necessaries, and totally void of all the comforts of life, except an inimitable degree of patience, for which he deserves a thousand times better fate... .

Discouraged by his experience, Bartram returned to Philadelphia within a year where he again tried his hand at business and failed. It was clear that Bartram the botanist was not cut out for the world of trade.

In marked contrast to William Bartram's commercial failures was his artistic success. "Billy's elegant drawings are admired by all who see them," observed Peter Collinson, who took great interest in displaying the young man's drawings to other influential persons. "I have shown thy performances to many, who deservedly admire and commend them, in hopes to find encouragement..." he wrote. Among those with whom Collinson shared Bartram's sketches were Georg Dionysius Ehret, then England's leading flower painter, the Duchess of Portland, "a great virtuoso" who agreed to "bestow twenty guineas on his performances, for a trial," and Dr John Fothergill, who would play such an important role in supporting William's career. Collinson described the fateful introduction in a letter of 1768:

This morning, Doctor Fothergill came and breakfasted here. As I am always thoughtful how to make BILLY'S ingenuity turn to some advantage, I bethought of showing the Doctor his last elegant performances. He deservedly admired them, and thinks so fine a pencil is worthy of encouragement; and BILLY may value himself on having such a fine patron, who is eminent for his generosity, and his noble spirit to promote every branch in Natural History. He desires BILLY would employ some of his time in drawing all the Land, River, and Sea Shells, from the very smallest to the largest; when very small, eight or six in a half sheet, as they grow larger, six or four, then two or one, without any shade, which oftentime confounds the shape of the shell. Note the place where found, and add if anything peculiar to them besides.

He is not in haste, and desires nothing may be done in a hurry. When two or three shells are done, send them when there is convenient opportunity.

The introduction could not have been made at a more auspicious moment, for Peter Collinson would not live out the year.

In John Fothergill, William found a generous, supportive patron whose interests were as wide and varied as his own. At a time when the flora and fauna of North America was still largely undiscovered, John Fothergill was already looking ahead to the possibility of species extinction. In a letter of 1770 suggesting that William make drawings of "the rest of your American tortoises," Fothergill observed:

As the [human] inhabitants increase, the species of this and other animals, as well as vegtables, will, perhaps, be extinguished, or exist only in some still distant parts. It would, therefore, be of great advantage to natural history, to have everything of a fugitive nature consigned to paper, with as much accuracy as possible.

Fothergill's desire for exhaustive documentation of American wildlife and his willingness to pay "proper compensation" for anything Bartram could draw, collect, or describe, made him the ideal patron.

Having made no progress with a business career in Philadelphia, William returned to Cape Fear, North Carolina in 1770. From there he continued his correspondence with Fothergill, sending him plants and drawings as requested. In the fall of 1772, Bartram wrote his patron with an ambitious proposal: like his father before him, William Bartram wished to make an expedition to Florida.

Fothergill admired William's talent and "relish for natural history" and hated to see "such a genius... sink under distress". He wrote that he believed such a search would "be of use to science in general" and that he hoped that at least some of the plants William discovered could "grow anywhere" and so be introduced to cultivation in England. Fothergill agreed to pay Bartram fifty pounds per year (the stipend John Bartram had received from the King for his Florida trip) plus shipping expenses and a bonus for each painting he sent.

William Bartram's wanderings those four years in the Southeast are complex and confusing, for unlike later American exploratory trips, Bartram had no predetermined destination. Instead, he meandered back and forth through the country as his inclination and fortunes dictated. While a good deal of his time was spent along the east coast in South Carolina, Georgia, and Florida, where he returned to many of the sites visited on his 1765-66 trip with his father, William Bartram reached as far west as Pointe Coupee on the Mississippi. *En route*, along the Gulf Coast, the naturalist was struck down by a nearly fatal illness (possibly scarlet fever) that left him severely weakened and partially blind. Elsewhere on his journey, he faced harrowing alligator attacks, hostile Indians, and a multitude of other dangers. In his account of the trip, however, Bartram tends to stress the glories of his experience and the wonder of nature. Unlike later field naturalists for example Constantine Rafinesque (1783-1840) and David Douglas (1798-1834), whose journals are filled with detailed accounts of their own hardships, Bartram's writings are consistently positive and optimistic.

Bartram saw the world as "a glorious apartment of the boundless palace of the sovereign Creator", with its various components vegetable, animal, and mineral, reflective of "the almighty power, wisdom, and beneficience of the Supreme Creator and Sovereign Lord of the Universe". His interesting blend of traditional Quaker thought, scientific inquiry, and Pantheism (the worship of nature as a symbol of God), successfully bridged the gap between the eighteenth and nineteenth centuries; between Enlightenment explanation and Romantic perception.

Ironically, Bartram's philosophical and religious beliefs also helped him to see ecological relationships between various parts of the natural world that had not been recognized previously and would not be emphasized again until the nineteenth century. Although he frequently analyzed individual components of nature in detail, he never lost sight of the larger— divinely created—order of life. Bartram's ecological perception of the world is well illustrated in his description of a struggle between a "bomble bee" and a garden spider. After a fifteen minute battle, observed Bartram in the introduction to his book, the bee "expired in the arms of the devouring spider, who, ascending the rope with his game, retired to feast on it under cover of leaves; and perhaps before night became himself the delicious evening repast of a bird or lizard". Bartram believed that each part of nature was "designed for different purposes and uses", and that the attributes of each were "of sufficient importance to manifest the divine and inevitable workmanship" of the Creator. This view, which extended to the differing races of man, was quite different from the hierarchical perception of the world held by many of his non-Quaker contemporaries.

Bartram's comprehensive documentation of his four-year trip was recommended by John Fothergill who suggested that it would "be right to keep a little journal, marking the soil, situation, plants in general, remarkable animals, where found, and the general particulars relative to them...". He further requested that this journal, or series of journals, be sent to Charleston "when it can be done safely... least they should be lost or stolen, which would be an irretrievable loss."

The original journals which served as the basis for Bartram's *Travels* have since suffered the irretrievable loss Fothergill had feared. Two documents describing the trip in Bartram's own hand, have survived, however, and are today in the British Museum (Natural History).

These manuscripts, which cover the first two years of Bartram's trip (1773-1774), were presumably copied (or paraphased) from the naturalist's field notes during the expedition and shipped to Fothergill in London. While they lack the polish and detail of the *Travels*, they contain many of the same evocative descriptions of the terrain and provide a fascinating insight into Bartram's perceptions and methods of expression.

If Bartram's original field journals had survived (and they may yet come to light), they would give us an even better understanding of his trip and his skill as a writer. By comparing the day to day entries with the published account of his travels, we would be able to witness first hand the careful crafting of a travel log into an epic.

Nowhere has Bartram indicated that he originally had a publication in mind when he set off on his four-year trip, but as several of John Bartram's travel journals had been published abroad, the younger explorer probably considered such a possibilty. The second of the two journal volumes at the British Museum (Natural History) contains a number of spelling, grammatical, and taxonomic corrections, indicating that Bartram reworked the manuscript with the aid of a dictionary and a copy of Linnaeus's *Systema Naturae* (1766-1768) before sending it on to Fothergill in London. While this evidence of minor editorial revision may simply reflect Bartram's desire to please his highly educated patron, it may also hint of an early interest in preparing his notes for a broader audience.

A letter from naturalist Johann David Schoepf, who visited Philadelphia in 1783, mentions Bartram's "unprinted manuscript on the nations and products" of Florida. When the manuscript may have been first ready for publication, however, we do not know. The earliest public reference to a book by Bartram appears in a broadside issued by Philadelphia publisher Enoch Story, Jr in 1786, inviting subscriptions to a planned edition of the *Travels*. This proposal evidently foundered, for it was another Philadelphia firm, James and Johnson, which eventually published the book. James and Johnson began a national advertising and sales campaign for *Travels* in 1790, successfully securing subscriptions from President Washington, Vice President Adams, Thomas Jefferson and other notables. Within a year they were able to publish the book.

It is difficult to explain the fourteen-year delay between Bartram's return from the South and publication of his *Travels*. He was no doubt quite busy with matters relating to his father's botanical garden (which John had deeded to William's younger brother John, Jr in 1771 but with which William was also actively involved after his father's death in 1777). It is also possible that William's shy and retiring nature caused him to refrain from any venture that might attract unwelcome notoriety. Only after the prompting of his ambitious young friend, Benjamin Smith Barton (who actually offered to co-author the *Travels*), do we see evidence of Bartram's willingness to publish.

Perhaps the most important factor in delaying Bartram from issuing an account of the trip, however, was his uncompromising dedication to scientific accuracy. For years he waited in vain for confirmation from England on the proper nomenclature for the many new plants he had discovered. Daniel Carl Solander and other British enthusiasts were so busy trying to classify the hundreds of new plants then coming in from the South Pacific (where Captain James Cook and others had caught the attention of the scientific world) that they had little time to devote to the less dramatic specimens of southeastern North America, especially those collected by a botanist they had never met and whose appreciation would do little to advance their own stature in the competitive world of eighteenth century academia.

Although Bartram rarely complained of it, the European neglect of his discoveries proved doubly harmful, for it not only denied Bartram the knowledge he sought to share, but it permitted others to publish, and thereby receive credit for, the discovery of plants and animals Bartram had sent to England years before. By 1791, when the *Travels* finally appeared, many of Bartram's most important biological finds had already been described in other books—often by naturalists who had learned of them from Bartram himself and who felt no need for European concurrence on their indentification. Since the first published describer of each new species receives credit for its discovery, Bartram lost recognition for much of his pioneering work.

Despite the timing of the *Travels*' publication, the scientific value of the work was widely recognized at home and abroad. "The amateur of natural science cannot fail of being highly gratified by the perusal of this volume", wrote a reviewer in the *Massachusetts Magazine*. "Mr Bartram has accurately described a variety of birds, fish and reptiles, hitherto but little known: His botanical researches are more copious than any other writers with whom we are acquainted." Many interested readers wrote to Bartram and others to discuss the significance of his biological finds.

Bartram's unusual literary style was less highly regarded. The author's "rapturous effusions" were considered by some excessive and detrimental to the book. One critical American reviewer considered the style "very incorrect and disgustingly pompous"; another found it "too luxuriant and florid to merit the palm of chastity and correctness".

The flowery passages in *Travels*, which attracted such criticism, were quite alien to the literary tastes of the period. His descriptions of the setting sun, for example, parted conspicuously from the restrained, analytical style more typical of his day:

> How glorious the powerful sun, Minister of the Most High, in the rule and government of this earth, leaves our hemisphere, retiring from our sight beyond the western forests! I behold with gratitude his departing smiles, tugging the fleecy roseate clouds, now riding far away on the Eastern horizon; behold they vanish from sight in the azure skies!... The glorious sovereign of day, calling in his bright beaming emanations, leaves us in his absence to the milder government and protection of the silver queen of night, attended by millions of brilliant luminaries... .

Despite such occasional outbursts of poetic revelry, Bartram did temper most of his writing with objective observation. "The attention of a traveller should be particularly turned", he explained in his introduction, "to the various works of Nature, to mark the distinctions of the climates he may explore and to offer such useful observations on the different productions as may occur... . How far the writer of the following sheets has succeeded in furnishing information on these subjects, the reader will be capable of determining." If anything, the balance of subjective and objective analysis is what distinguishes Bartram's writing from that of his more conservative contemporaries.

Not surprisingly, as tastes changed over time, so did critical assessment of Bartram's style. A French reviewer of 1799 found his descriptions neither too dry nor too exaggerated, but "correct" and even "elegant". Mid-nineteenth century American critics, by then accustomed to romantic writing and emotional expression in prose, were even more enthusiastic about Bartram's writing and fully endorsed the *Travels* as literature.

For whatever reasons, the first edition of *Travels* met with only limited sales in the United States and was not reprinted here until 1928. In Europe, however, the book met a much more favorable reception. A 1792 London edition was quickly followed by a second edition there, and by editions in Dublin (1793), Berlin (1793), Vienna (1793), Haarlem (1794–1797), Amsterdam (1797), and Paris (1799 and 1801).

"Anthropology and ethnology have been considerably enriched by our author", enthused the editor of the 1793 Berlin edition:

But natural history proper receives the most important enrichment through this work.... He acquaints us with a considerable number of new plants.... The fauna has also gained much through him, both through the discovery of several hitherto unknown or doubtful species and reports on the migratory birds and on the life histories of large injurious animals, such as the Rattlesnake and the Alligator... . Especially he exhibits in the whole long journey fortitude, courage, and quiet endurance of all kinds of discomforts and dangers, whereby he is distinguished above many other travelers.

For readers (and writers) of the coming Romantic period, the benign and fantastic world Bartram described was the Eden for which man had long been searching. The American Indians, whose natural order he revealed, suggested pleasant images of man before the fall.

Samuel Taylor Coleridge considered the *Travels* "a work of high merit [in] every way" and copied sections of the book into his own notebook for further study. He later adopted many of Bartram's images for use in such works as *The Rime of the Ancient Mariner*, *Osorio*, *Kubla Khan*, *Frost at Midnight*, *This Lime-tree Bower My Prison* and *Lewti*. Similarly, William Wordsworth drew ideas and images from Bartram's *Travels* for use in *Ruth*, *The Prelude*, *The Excursion*, *A Guide Through the Lake District* and the *Ecclesiastical Sonnets*. Further study of Bartram's impact on writers of the nineteenth century is needed to reveal the full extent of his influence.

The many editions and translations of the *Travels* to appear abroad within a few years of its first publication helped to make Bartram one of the most widely read American authors in Europe at the close of the eighteenth and opening of the nineteenth centuries. Despite this success, Bartram published only two other articles during his lifetime: "Anecdotes of an American Crow", *Philadelphia Medical and Physical Journal*, 1804, and "Observations on the Pea Fly or Beetle, and Fruit Curculio", *Memoirs of the Philadelphia Society for the Promotion of Agriculture*, 1808. A third treatise, on the Creek and Cherokee Indian, was not published until 1851.

Bartram may have been discouraged by skeptical reviews his *Travels* received from American critics. He was particularly sensitive to the criticism of his accounts of alligator attack. One English visitor recalled that in 1794, when "joking the old gentleman about the alligators that he had formerly fought with, he became so reserved that we could get but little conversation from him". Although he complained to fellow botanist William Baldwin of other errors in the *Travels* which "had not been published under his own inspection", Bartram defended the accuracy of his alligator observations to the end. The degree to which Bartram suffered personally from the criticism he received is poignantly revealed by Baldwin who "paid the venerable William Bartram a short visit" in the summer of 1817—Bartram was then seventy-eight:

> Aware of the suspicions which some entertain of his veracity, it was truly a feast to me to observe how his time-worn countenance brightened up at the vindication of his character which I informed him I was prepared to offer [after a visit to the same location].

Perhaps if such vindication and support had been offered earlier and expressed publicly, Bartram would have been spared the criticism and ridicule that caused him to become so publicly withdrawn during the closing years of his life.

While some American readers may not have been ready for Bartram's literary style, and harbored a skepticism about some of his observations, most were nonetheless appreciative of his breadth and depth of knowledge. In addition to inheriting his father's mantle as America's leading naturalist, Bartram, with his careful note taking, established a position as the country's most knowledgeable ornithologist and an authority on Indian culture. His familiarity with a wide range of natural history topics caused visitors from near and far to seek him out at the renowned garden at Kingsessing, four miles southwest of Philadelphia on the Schuylkill River.

During the Constitutional Convention of 1787, Alexander Hamilton, James Madison, John Rutledge, George Mason and a number of other delegates traveled to Kingsessing to visit Bartram. One of the visitors reported finding the naturalist in his garden "barefooted, hoe in hand, chopping at weeds". George Washington, another visitor, enjoyed his visit with Bartram, but found the garden considerably less formal than Mount Vernon. He remarked in his journal that the place "was not laid off with much taste".

Visitors like the French botanists André and François Michaux and American naturalists Benjamin Smith Barton, Thomas Nuttall, Frederick Pursh, Henry Muhlenberg, and Constantine Rafinesque were undoubtedly more interested in Bartram's knowledge than his taste. Their letters and published works frequently mention Bartram and his generosity in sharing specimens, information and ideas.

Bartram's two most frequent visitors during the final decades of his life were Thomas Say (1787–1834) his great-nephew, and Alexander Wilson (1766–1813), a Scottish immigrant who taught school not far from Bartram's home. For a while, Wilson actually lived with the Bartram family. Both men went on to establish themselves as scientists of world renown. Say, who retraced Bartram's southern travels in 1818, is today considered the father of American entomology and conchology. Wilson, who with Bartram's advice and guidance, produced the earliest definitive work on American birds, is today recognized as the father of American ornithology.

The transition between generations, as exemplified by these men, could not have been more dramatic. William Bartram had seen and described the world as a complex tapestry of interwoven parts. Lacking adequate support in America, he looked to Europe for initial instruction (through books), patronage, and scholarly approval. By contrast, the new generation of American scientists who sought his guidance were specialists focusing on individual parts of the overwhelming whole. By 1812 they had formed their own Academy of Natural Science (in Philadelphia) and were finding domestic support for their investigations.

Bartram, who was himself asked to participate in a federally-sponsored expedition to the West, seemed to understand and encourage these new waves of nationalism. By publishing the *Travels* in Philadelphia first (despite his many contacts abroad) and by accepting an invitation to membership in the Academy of Natural Sciences of Philadelphia soon after its founding, Bartram lent his endorsement to the national movement in American science. Had he accepted the University of Pennsylvania's invitation to teach botany in 1782, he might have made that final transition from eighteenth-century generalist to nineteenth-century specialist.

Bartram lived during an era of American exploration in which discoverers and reporters of discovery were by necessity often one and the same. Few, if any, of his contemporaries possessed the diverse range of talents, necessary to perform both roles as effectively as he. In his greatest legacy, the *Travels*, Bartram leaves us a unique account of eighteenth century America seen with the eye of an artist, recorded with the logic of a scientist and expressed with the words of a literary master.

In a letter to Ralph Waldo Emerson, written in 1851, Thomas Carlyle pointed out the change of attitude and perception so evident between his century and Bartram's. In so doing, he beautifully summarized the distinctive character of Bartram's *Travels* that makes this book the eighteenth century American classic that it is:

> Do you know Bartram's *Travels*? Treats of Florida chiefly, has a wonderful kind of floundering eloquence in it; and has grown immeasurable old. All American libraries ought to provide themselves with that kind of book; and keep them as a future biblical article.

N.B. This essay was originally published as an introduction to William Bartram's *Travels* published by Peregrine Smith Books, Salt Lake City, Utah, 1980. Copyright on the essay is held by Peregrine Smith, Inc. Permission has been granted to reprint. N. J. Root.

BOOKS FROM THE BARTRAM LIBRARY

Robert McCracken Peck
*The Academy of Natural Sciences,
19th and the Parkway,
Philadelphia, Pennsylvania 19103*

Both John and William Bartram were voracious readers, obtaining their books in exchange for plant specimens or as gifts of friendship from British and European correspondents. Because William lived in his family's house throughout his life (except when traveling in the South) it is safe to assume that his father's library was also his own.

Many books are mentioned in the correspondence of both Bartrams, giving an indication of how wide ranging their interests were. Of these most were probably borrowed from James Logan, a family friend whose private library was one of the largest in Philadelphia, from John Bartram's Friends Meeting, on whose Library Committee he served, or from the Library Company of Philadelphia, a private subscription library to which both men had access.

Despite such borrowing from other sources, internal evidence suggests that the Bartram's own library was quite a good one. Unfortunately, with time, it has been broken up and dispersed. A careful search of libraries in the United States has turned up the following books with an irrefutable Bartram provenance. It is hoped that the publication of this list may help to bring other books from the Bartram library to light.

Contributions to the History of North American Natural History. Society for the Bibliography of Natural History, London, 1983.

AITON, William
Hortus Kewensis, London, 1789.
Inscription: "For William Bartram from Robert Barclay 1790" and below
that "A present for Coll. Robert Carr from his affectionate friend and
relative William Bartram 1819."
Location: The Pennsylvania Horticultural Society, Philadelphia.

BARNES, Thomas
A New Method of Propagating Fruit-Trees... , Second Edition, London:
For R. Baldwin, and J. Jackson, 1759.
Manuscript signature of John Bartram "his book, given him by ... ?
Location: The Library Company of Philadelphia

BUFFON, George Louis Leclerc de
Natural History... , London: For W. Strahan, T. Cadell, and W. Creech,
1781.
Presentation copy from Benjamin Smith Barton to William Bartram.
Location: The Library Company of Philadelphia.

DALIBARD, Thomas Francois
Florae Parisiensis Prodromus ... , Paris: P. Alex Le Prieur for Durand
and Pisset, 1749.
John Bartram: This is one of two copies sent by Dalibard to Franklin (*vide*
Dalibard to BF, March 31, 1754), one of which was for John Bartram. This
was given to the Library Company of Philadelphia by Bartram.
Location: The Library Company of Philadelphia.

DARWIN, Erasmus
Phytologia ... , Dublin: For P. Byrne, 1800.
Presentation copy from Benjamin Smith Barton to William Bartram.
Location: The Library Company of Philadelphia.

DILLENIUS, John James
Historia Muscorum ..., Oxford: E. Theatro Sheldoniano, 1741.
John Bartram's bookplate; and inscribed on the fly-leaf "John Bartram His
Booke 1742 sent by Doctor Dillenius professor at Oxford." Presented to the
Library Company by John Bartram... April 17, 1773. Gift of Dellenius.
Location: The Library Company of Philadelphia.

GRONOVIUS, Johann Friederic
Index Supellectilis Lapidaea... , Leyden: for Cornelius Haak, 1750.
On Flyleaf: "The Gift of Mr. John Bartram."
Location: The Library Company of Philadelphia.

HILL, John
A History of Plants, 1751.
Signature of John Bartram. (For Bartram's observations on the book see his
letter to Peter Collinson of July, 1754, reprinted in Darlington's *Memorials*,
pp. 195–196.)
Location: Library of the Academy of Natural Sciences of Philadelphia.

HOME, Henry, Lord Kames
The Gentleman Farmer... , Edinburgh: For John Bell *et al*, 1788.
Presentation copy from Benjamin Smith Barton to John Bartram, Jr.
Location: The Library Company of Philadelphia.

JUSTICE, James
  The Scots Gardiners (sic) *Director... By a gentleman, one of the members of the Royal Society. The Second edition*, Edinburgh, 1759.
Manuscript note of inside front cover: "John Bartram His Booke being a present from Sir John St. Cleair 1761."
Location: University of Pennsylvania.

LINNAEUS, Carolus
  Caroli Linnaei Naturae Curiosorum Dioscoridis Secundi Systema Naturae..., Stockholme: Apud Gottfr. Kiesewetter, 1740.
Manuscript signature "John Bartram His Booke Sent to him by Doctor Gronovius in the year 1746."
Location: The Library Company of Philadelphia.

LINNAEUS, Carolus
  Genera plantarum.
Manuscript inscription "John Bartram, His Booke, sent to him by Doctor Gronovius."
Location: John Bartram House, Philadelphia c/o John Bartram Association.

LINNAEUS, Carolus
  Species plantarum, Second edition (1762-63).
Signatures of William Bartram on Flyleaf of Vol. 1, on verso of title page in Vol.2 and on p. 785 of Vol. 2.
Location: Library of the Academy of Natural Sciences of Philadelphia.

LINNAEUS, Carolus
  Systema naturae (1758).
Presentation copy to William Bartram from Dr Thomas T. Hewson of Philadelphia, dated 1808.
Location: Library of the Academy of Natural Sciences of Philadelphia.

LINNAEUS, Carolus
  Systema vegetabilium (1774).
Presentation copy to William Bartram from Doctor Keilman of Sweden, dated 1782; presented by William Bartram to James Bartram in 1804.
Location: Library of the Academy of Natural Sciences of Philadelphia.

MILLER, Joseph
  Botanicum Officinale of a Compendious Herbal: Giving an account of all such Plants as are now used in the practice of Physick with their Descriptions and Virtues. London: Printed for E. Bell, 1722.
Signature of Moses & William Bartram.
Location: The Library Company of Philadelphia.

MILLER, Phillip
  The Gardener's Dictionary, London: 1733-1739. 2 vols.
Both volumes have John Bartram bookplates. Vol. 1 has no signature, but a later note, not in his hand: "This volume was sent to John Bartram by Dr Dillenius." Vol. 2 has manuscript note: "John Bartram His Booke 1739, a present from the Right Honorable Lord Petre.
See William Darlington, (1849), *Memorials of John Bartram and Humphry Marshall*, Philadelphia 135, 376.

There is also a manuscript note about the sale of the volumes to Andrew M. Eastwick by Colonel Carr (identified as the husband of Bartram's granddaughter) in 1853.
Location: Presented to the University of Pennsylvania in 1914.

PEALE, Charles Willson
  A Scientific and Descriptive Catalogue... , Philadelphia: By Samuel H. Smith, 1796.
Presentation copy from Peale to William Bartram with signature.
Location: The Library Company of Philadelphia.

RAUWOLF, Leonard
  Flora Orientalis sive Recensio Plantarum... , Leyden: Wilhelm de Groot, 1755. Inscription "The Gift of Mr John Bartram" "Doc Gronovius to Mr John Bartram".
Location: The Library Company of Philadelphia.

RUSH, Benjamin
  Essays, Literary, Moral & Philosophical... , Philadelphia: Printed by Thomas & Samuel F. Bradford, 1798.
Signature of William Bartram.
Location: The Library Company of Philadelphia.

SLOANE, Sir Hans
  Catalogus Plantarum quae in Insula Jamaica Sponte proveniunt... Seu Prodromi Historiae Naturalis Jamaica Par Prima, London: D. Brown, 1696.
Signature of John Bartram.
Location: The Library Company of Philadelphia.

SLOANE, Sir Hans
  A Voyage to the Islands Madera, Barbados, Nieves, S. Christophers and Jamaica, London, 1725, 2 vols.
Both bear Bartram's signature: "John Bartram his book. A present from Sir Hans Sloan 1742" and his bookplate.
Location: Boston Public Library.

SMELLIE, William
  The Philosophy of Natural History, Philadelphia: For Robert Campbell, 1791.
Presentation copy of book from Nicholas Collin, 1800, to William Bartram; and to James Bartram, 1813.
Location: The Library Company of Philadelphia.

  The Spectator, Glasgow: By A. Duncan and Company, For James Knox *et al.*, 1767. In Eight Volumes... Vol. VII.
Signature of John Bartram "his book and han(d)."
Location: The Library Company of Philadelphia.

VAILLANT, Paul *et al.*
  A New Introduction to Trade... , London. 1758.
Presentation copy of book from Peter Collinson to William Bartram with signature.
Location: The Library Company of Philadelphia.

WILSON, Alexander
American Ornithology, Philadelphia: 1804–1814. Nine Volumes.
The first volume has a blank leaf at the front with the following insciption:
"To Wm. Bartram
    of Kingsess Botanic Gardens.
        A present from the Author
                                (and below that)
    This vol. with the whole sett of nine Vol.
    Is presented by her Unkle William Bartram, to
    his esteemed nie(c or s)e Ann B. Carr
                        William Bartram
                        November 20th, 1815.
The eight succeeding volumes are inscribed:
"To Ann B. Carr
    From her Unkle
    William Bartram"
Location: Rare Book Department, The Free Library of Philadelphia.

JOHN GOULD IN AMERICA

Gordon C. Sauer
6400 Prospect Avenue,
Kansas City, Mo. 64132.

There are two valid reasons for giving a paper to the first North American meeting of the Society on the subject of John Gould in America. The first reason is that it is especially fitting at this premier North American meeting of a Society that was founded in London, to provide another link between England and North America. And the second reason is that very few people know that the London ornithologist, John Gould, visited America.

Gould indeed did come to America. He came in 1857, with his son Charles, and they visited New York City, Philadelphia, Washington, Cleveland, Buffalo, Niagara Falls (of course), Toronto, Montreal, Boston, New Haven, and then returned to New York City. They spent forty days here.

Gould was born in 1804 in the fishing village of Lyme Regis in Dorset, England. When he was 14 his father was appointed as a gardener at the Royal Gardens in Windsor. During these years Gould apparently acquired quite a proficiency in taxidermy. By the age of 20 or so, he had moved to London and established himself on Bruton Street as a taxidermist. There is an extant bill in the Windsor Castle Archives to the King of England, George IV, "for preserving a Thick knee'd Bustard £1.5.0". This bill is dated 1825 when Gould was 21. Additional bills show Gould did a considerable amount of taxidermy for the King over the next five years.

At the age of 23 Gould was appointed the first "Curator and Preserver" for the newly formed Zoological Society of London.

The combination then of his access to unusual bird speciments, and his marriage to a woman with artistic talent opened the door for a well-conceived publishing venture. His first work was an imperial folio volume on birds of the Himalaya mountains. It consisted of 80 hand-colored lithographic plates containing 100 specimens of birds—a century of birds. N. A. Vigors wrote this text but in future works Gould was responsible for the text.

Gould's role in the publishing venture was not as the artist. He did draw very tolerable rough sketches of birds in the positions he wished them displayed. His wife was the initial artist, then later she was joined by Edward Lear (of Nonsense rhyme fame). After Gould's wife's death from child-bed fever in 1841, H. C. Richter assumed the artist's task, then William Hart and Joseph Wolf. Gould, with these talented assistants, was able over a fifty year period until his death in 1881, to publish 20 major imperial folio works in 50 volumes, eighteen works on birds of the world, and two on the mammals of Australia. They were illustrated with over 3,000 hand-colored lithographs.

Contributions to the History of North American Natural History. Society for the Bibliography of Natural History, London, 1983.

Gould is the Audubon of Australia. In 1838 Gould, with his wife, eldest son, and fellow collector, John Gilbert, travelled to the colony of Australia. During 19 months there he collected over 300 new species or sub-species of birds. He made every moment count, even on board ship he observed and collected oceanic birds. When they returned to England in August 1840 they had circumnavigated the globe.

By 1857 when Gould came to America he was definitely established as the most prominent British and Australian ornithologist, with an international reputation. He was 52 years old.

Gould ostensibly came to America to see a live hummingbird. He had begun a detailed study of this species in the late 1840s. His famous *Monograph of the ... Humming-birds* was begun in 1849, to be completed in 1861. But, anyone who studies the life of John Gould knows that he also came to America to get new subscribers for his works. An ancillary reason was to make additional scientific acquaintances so that he could obtain and share bird specimens.

Soon after his arrival in New York City Gould wrote to his family in London:

New York
16th May 57

My dearest children,
    I take the earliest opportunity after arriving to say we are well, in a day or two either Charles or myself will write more fully. Indeed it is just probable that our second letter may arrive first. The entrance to New York from the sea is truly beautiful and from what I have seen of the place (I mean the city) I am not a little astonished and amused. I trust in a day or two to change this turmoil for quieter scenes in a state of nature. Trusting my dearest children that you are all well and that a kind providence will ever protect you. I will ask you to kindly remember me to Miss Yates, Mr Prince, and all enquiring friends, and believe me to remain, my dear children,

Your ever affectionate father,
John Gould

A copy of this letter was sent to me in 1954 by the late Alec Chisholm of Australia. He had obtained it from the Gould descendants in England in 1938. The original letter is now in the Spencer Library at the University of Kansas, as part of the largest collection in the world of Gouldiana, begun by Ralph Ellis. (The library contains a complete set of Gould's works, many in the original parts as issued, and, most importantly, over 1,500 of Gould's and his artists' original drawings.)

Additional information on Gould and his son's arrival appeared in the New York *Evening Post* of Friday, 15 May 1857, on page 2: "Passengers by the Asia ... Gould, Gould, Jr.".

The most important news in New York City for Saturday, 16 May was this arrival of the *Asia*. As reported in the *Daily Times*, "The British Mail Steamer *Asia*, from Liverpool, 3 o'clock afternoon of Saturday, May 2, arrived yesterday morning". Then follows eight columns of world news brought over on the *Asia*. Further on in this paper is the information that the "*Asia* ... passed 3 icebergs.".

While in New York City he met George N. Lawrence, a prominent American ornithologist. In Gould's *Monograph of the Trochilidae* ... or *Humming Birds*, volume 5, plate 297, the text for the Brilliant-fronted Emerald, contains this statement: "The specimen described was presented to me by G. N. Lawrence, Esq. when I visited New York in 1858 [1857]". In future years Lawrence served as Gould's American agent.

The next evidence of Gould's trip to America was his presence at an ordinary meeting of the Academy of Sciences of Philadelphia on 19 May 1857. Gould was listed in the minutes of this meeting as being a Corresponding Member.[1] He had been elected to this membership on 31 January 1843. Dr T. B. Wilson was in the chair and it was Wilson who, in 1847 through his brother, Edward, purchased for the Philadelphia Academy Gould's collection of over 1,800 specimens of Australian birds, including the type specimens from Gould's Australian exploration. The cost was £1,000 or around $5,000. The British Museum had turned down Gould's offer to sell the Australian bird and egg collection to them. Witmer Stone[2] and Rodolphe Meyer de Schauensee[3] have written extensively about this collection.

This 19 May 1857 Philadelphia Academy meeting was also attended by "Messrs. Leidy [Joseph Leidy, M. D.], A. [Aubrey] H. Smith [attorney], Corse [Dr B. M. Corse], W. S. Wilson, J. D. [Dickinson] Sergeant [attorney], Draper [Lyman Draper], J. A. [Aitkin] Meigs [M. D.], Woodhouse [Dr Samuel Washington Woodhouse], Schafhirt [Frederick Schafhirt, entomologist], Morris [Dr J. C. Morris, ichthyologist], Rand [B. Howard Rand, M. D., Recording Secretary]," in addition to Dr Thomas Bellerby Wilson and John Gould. The elaboration on these names was obtained from the index and text of the 1857 and 1858 Proceedings of the Academy of Natural Sciences of Philadelphia.

Gould wrote in his five volume Humming-bird work (vol. 3, pl. 131, the account of the Ruby-throated Humming-bird) of his stay in Philadelphia where, to his great delight, he finally saw a live hummingbird in Bartram's Gardens. He was accompanied by William Baily.

Two more items concerning Gould in Philadelphia are relevant. The first is that the Philadelphia photographic establishment of J. E. McClees made a portrait of Gould. This portrait is in three states in the Library of the Academy.

Secondly, while in Philadelphia Gould made a pencil sketch of a bird which resembles the Yellow-billed Cuckoo. (Item 4 in Collection 71, MSS 94 in vault, Library, ANSP.) The notation (in Baily's hand?) on the drawing states "Sketched by Mr John Gould of London/at this Academy May 1857." It is my opinion that this is the *only* drawing of a bird definitely attributable to John Gould since it was done in Philadelphia when he had none of his artists around him.[4]

There is also a more finely finished water-color pencilled sketch of a hummingbird in the Library of the Philadelphia Academy. (Item 6, in Collection 71, MS 912.) In Gould's hand appears this note: "Original rough design/J. Gould/May 9, 1849/given at the request of Mr Wilson." Edward Wilson apparently also wanted an *original* drawing by John Gould. I also feel that this hummingbird water-color is a true example of Gould's not insignificant artistry, but of course he could have had one of his London artists assist in this drawing.

On 23 May a note appeared in the Washington *Evening Star:* "Arrivals at the Hotels... Willards' Hotel... Mr Gould, son, Eng."

Gould wrote in his *"An Introduction to the... Humming-Birds* (page 12) that "some friends at Washington (Baron Osten Sacken, Mr Odo Russell, and his brother Mr Arthur Russell)... captured for me... a *Trochilus colubris* [Ruby-throated Hummingbird]." The hummingbird "immediately afterwards partook of some saccharine food that was presented to it, and in two hours it pumped the fluid out of a little bottle whenever I offered it; and in this way it lived with me a constant companion for several days, travelling in a little thin gauzy bag distended by a slender piece of whalebone, and suspended to a button of my coat."

In Washington Gould also met Spencer Fullerton Baird, Assistant Secretary of the Smithsonian Institution, Joseph Henry, Secretary of the Smithsonian, James Buchanan, the President of the United States, and Lord Napier, the new British Ambassador to the United States. Lord Francis Napier had come over from England on the *Asia* with the Goulds.

This latter information comes from two main sources. The first is a series of fourteen communications between Gould and Baird which reside in the Library of the Smithsonian Institution Archives (Secretary Letters) beginning with a letter from Gould from Toronto on 3 June 1857, and ending on 31 January 1864, with a letter from Gould in London.

The second source is a fortunate find. It is a long letter from Charles Gould, his 23 year old son, to the family at home, written on 11 June 1857 from Boston. In this letter Charles writes many interesting facts and anecdotes about their whirlwind journey, and he also lists an itinerary! The letter is part of the collection of Dr Geoffrey Edelsten of Winchester, England, great-grandson of John Gould.

Here are further dates and places on their American journey from these two sources or other sources.

The Goulds' trip from Washington to Cleveland *via* Altoona, Pennsylvania, as related in Charles's letter was apparently accomplished by back-tracking by rail to Baltimore from Washington on the Baltimore and Ohio Railroad, and then taking the Pennsylvania Railroad to Altoona and on to Cleveland on Lake Erie.[5]

Assuming a stay of four days in Washington, this would mean they left Washington on 27 of May. Allowing a day to go to Cleveland, they possibly arrived on 28 May.

In 1857 an organization of naturalists did exist in Cleveland, the Cleveland Academy of Natural Sciences. The minutes of their meetings are incomplete, but there is no record of Gould's visit.[6]

Gould mentioned in his 3 June letter to S. F. Baird "What an excellent man I found in Dr Kirtland". Dr Jared P. Kirtland was the leading natural scientist in Cleveland, and Gould evidently did meet him.

If one assumes a stay of a day or two in Cleveland they probably arrived in Buffalo around 30 May. Mr Everard Palmer of Buffalo was a subscriber for Gould's five volume *Monograph of the Trochilidae, or Family of Humming Birds*.[7] Undoubtedly Gould met Palmer on this 1857 journey. In 1865 Palmer gave this Hummingbird set to the library of the Buffalo Society of Natural Sciences and by 1875 Palmer and Coleman T. Robinson had further contributed Gould's five volume *Birds of Great Britain*, three volume *Mammals of Australia*, and one volume each of *Partridges of America, Toucans* (1854) and *Trogons* (1875).

How long Gould and son stayed in Buffalo is unknown. There are no references to them in the Buffalo *Morning Express* or the *Evening News* around the dates of 30 May to 2 June.

They then proceeded to Niagara Falls. Charles Gould wrote in his letter regarding Niagara Falls that he was *not* disappointed in them. However, "there being no Humming Birds in the neighbourhood, and no savants, Mr Gould found the beauty of the falls alone insufficient to attract him more than a few hours, so off we started again... (Sic vita Gouldi Johnni)". One of Gould's descendants has a bracelet made from gold coins, purchased when they were at Niagara Falls. Charles continued "From Niagara we went partly by rail and partly by boat to Toronto".

On 3 June John Gould and son were in Toronto. Gould wrote Baird on that date: "... What an excellent man I found in Dr Kirtland [of Cleveland] — at Buffalo I also found some kind spirits.

I believe all my works will be taken at an institution in town [Buffalo] besides copies of the Humming Birds for private subscribers.

Here in Toronto many others are already ordered and among them a complete series bound in the best manner for the "Library of Parliament...".".

Dr James Bovell also wrote in the *Canadian Journal of Industry, Science and Art* (**2**: 328) that:

During the present summer we were visited by Mr John Gould, the distinguished Naturalist, whose chief object in his tour through Canada was for the purpose of studying the habits and manners of the species of *Trochilus* frequenting this portion of the North American Continent. Shortly after his return to England, at a meeting of the London Zoological Society, Mr Gould detailed some of the result of his observations. He arrived in Canada just before the period of the migration of these beautiful little birds from Mexico to the north, and had ample opportunities for observing them in a state of nature. Their actions he described as very peculiar and quite different from those of all other birds; the flight is performed by a motion of the wings so rapid as to be almost imperceptible; indeed, the muscular power of this little creature appears to be very great in every respect, as independently of its rapid and sustained flight, it grasps the small twigs, flowers, etc., upon which it alights with the utmost tenacity. It appears to be most active in the morning and evening, and to pass the middle of the day in a state of sleepy torpor. Occasionally it occurs in such numbers that fifty or sixty may be seen in a single tree. When captured it so speedily becomes tame that it will feed from the hand or mouth within half an hour. Mr Gould having been successful in keeping one alive in a gauze bag attached to his breast button for three days, during which it readily fed from a small bottle filled with a syrup of brown sugar and water, he determined to make an attempt to bring some living examples to England, in which he succeeded, but unfortunately they did not long survive their arrival; had they lived, it was his intention to have sent them to the Zoological Society's gardens, where they would doubtless have been objects of great attraction.

Mr Gould exhibited a highly interesting species of *Ceriornis*, which he had found in the collection of Dr Cabot, of Boston, who, with great liberality, permitted him to take it to England for the purpose of comparison and description. For this new bird, forming the fourth species of the genus, Mr Gould proposes the name of *Ceriornis Caboti*''.

This account was obviously written by Bovell after Gould had returned to England. He mentions Gould's presentation at the Zoological Society of London on 14 July 1857, regarding his visit to Boston and the *Ceriornis* specimen loaned him by Dr Cabot. The wording in Bovell's statement is almost identical to that written in the Proceedings of the Zoological Society of London for that meeting.

It might be assumed that the Goulds were in Toronto 3, 4, and 5 June and according to Charles's letter they attended "one or two dinner parties and... an evening at Government House".

Montreal was the next stop. Charles wrote that they stayed with Mr Hodges "one of the engineers of the Grand Trunk R.R. He was a fellow passenger of ours in the *Asia*." William D'Urban also reported to the Montreal Natural History Society (Society Minutes 1857) that "the celebrated Ornithologist Mr Gould F.R.S.... paid Montreal a flying visit of 3 or 4 days" at the beginning of June, and the dates could have been 6–9 June. Gould later wrote Baird that he had also met Dr John Rae, the explorer, when he was in Montreal.

According to Charles, they proceeded to Boston *via* Portland, and he wrote his detailed family letter on 11 June from Boston.

Concerning Boston, Gould reported to the Zoological Society of London on his return that he had met Dr Cabot "who with the greatest liberality, permitted him to bring... a highly interesting species of *Ceriornis*... to England for the purpose of comparison and description." Gould described it and named it *Ceriornis Caboti* at the 14 July 1857 meeting of the Zoological Society of London.[9]

The Goulds also stopped at Yale College in New Haven, Connecticut, on their way back to New York. On 19 November 1857, after Gould's return to London, he wrote to both Edward C. Herrick, the Yale College Librarian, and to Professor James D. Dana. To Herrick he wrote "I have the pleasure of sending you by the *Kangaroo* to New York, carefully packed, a box containing a copy of my work on the Humming Birds so far as published as ordered by your President when I had the pleasure of visiting Yale College in June last". To Dana he wrote "As I mentioned to you I am quite ready to forward a donation of 50 skins of birds... and you only have to say if they would be acceptable...". Gould also wished to be remembered "to the Messrs. Silliman Father and Son".

In the third and last letter of this Yale series, dated 12 February 1858, Gould was gratified to learn of the safe arrival of parts 1 to 14 of his work on the *Trochilidae*. Gould had also sent to Yale part 1 of his *Mammals of Australia* since Professor Dana had expressed an interest in having it purchased. Yale declined his offer, so Gould wrote that the part could be returned to G. N. Lawrence of New York City. Thus, Lawrence was already acting as Gould's agent in North America, as definitely revealed in the extant Gould-Lawrence correspondence beginning on the later date of 11 July 1868.

Gould's offer of fifty specimens of birds to Yale is interesting but not unusual. He would often sweeten the pot for a purchaser by offering bird specimens as a gift. Fred C. Sibley, Chief Museum Curator, of the Peabody Museum at Yale was able to supply copies of the pages of the catalog entries for Gould's donations and discovered that 23 of Gould's specimens were still identifiable as such.

A letter to Baird on 18 June from the Brevoort Hotel, which stood at the corner of 8th Street and Fifth Avenue, was undoubtedly written when they returned to New York City. Several more letters through 22 June were written to Baird. In them Gould mentioned the two naturalists, John Cassin of Philadelphia and George Lawrence of New York City, he also requested the skin of a humming-bird *Trochilus alexanderi*, and he made an offer to get desired specimens for Baird. A taxidermist in New York City by the name of Bell was referred to several times. In the letter of 22 June to Baird, Gould said he was leaving New York City in two days. On 24 June, according to the New York *Evening Post* "cleared this forenoon... Steamship Kangaroo, Jeffry, Liverpool — John G. Dale". Undoubtedly this is the boat they used to return to Liverpool and England.

Gould, in his *An Introduction to the Humming Birds*, p. 13, wrote: "The vessel in which I made the passage took a northerly course, which carried us over the banks of Newfoundland." (Incidentally, he attributed the death of the live hummingbirds he had with him to his cold weather exposure.)

On 14 July Gould attended the Zoological Society of London meeting, as stated before, and "detailed the results of his observations... [on] the habits and manners of the species Trochilus frequenting that portion of the American continent" in which he had travelled.

Gould's Australian birds and eggs had preceded him to America. Little could he realize, however, when on his American trip, that eighty years later the major contents of his workrooms in London, his rough sketches, his artists original drawings, and even a few lithographic stones, would also travel to America to have a final resting place in Lawrence, Kansas. They had been purchased from Henry Sotheran, Ltd of London by Ralph Ellis.

ACKNOWLEDGEMENTS

I would like to acknowledge the assistance of the following individuals and institutions: Venia T. Phillips, Martha T. Pilling, Anita Loscalzo, Sylva Baker and Carol M. Spawn of the Library of the Academy of Natural Sciences of Philadelphia; William A. Deiss of the Smithsonian Institution Archives; Mrs Mary Baum of the Cleveland Museum of Natural History; Dr Robert F. Andrle of the Buffalo Society of Natural Sciences; Patrick W. Gabor of the Buffalo and Erie County Historical Society; Donald E. Loker, Brydges Public Library of Niagara Falls; W. E. Swinton of Massey College, Toronto; Mrs Rachel Grover of the Thomas Fisher Rare Book Library of the University of Toronto; Eleanor MacLean, Blacker-Wood Librarian, McGill University, Montreal; Dr Roy Forsey and Dr E. H. Bensley of Montreal; Fred C. Sibley, Peabody Museum, Yale University; Suzanne L. Rutter, Beinecke Rare Book and Manuscript Library, Yale University; and, finally, Alexandra Mason and L. E. James Helyar and staff at the Kenneth Spencer Research Library at the University of Kansas.

Of course, none of my work on John Gould could have been accomplished without the very ready and kind assistance from the Gould descendants, especially Dr Geoffrey Edelsten of Winchester.

NOTES AND REFERENCES

[1] Library, Academy of Natural Sciences of Philadelphia, minutes of meeting, 1857. Collection 502, meeting of 19 May 1857.

[2] Stone, Witmer, with Mathews, G. M., 1913 A list of the species of Australian birds described by John Gould, with the location of the type-specimens. *Australian Avian Record* 1: 129–180.

[3] Meyer de Schauensee, Rodolphe, 1957 On some avian types, principally Gould's, in the collection of the Academy. *Proceeedings of the Academy of Natural Sciences of Philadelphia* **109**: 123–246.

[4] Sauer, G. C., 1976 John Gould, Artist? Testimony of the Yellow-billed Cuckoo. *Books and Libraries at the University of Kansas* 13(2): 8–11.

[5] Moody, John, 1919 *The chronicles of America...* Vol. 38. *The railroad builders*. New Haven.

[6] Cleveland Academy of Natural Sciences, 1874. *Proceedings of the Cleveland Academy of Natural Sciences, 1845 to 1859*. Cleveland.

[7] Gould, John, 1870 [Prospectus of the works on ornithology, etc. by John Gould, F.R.S. (with a list of subscribers to, or possessors of, the works.)]. London.

[8] Buffalo Society of Natural Sciences, 1938 *Seventy-five years*. Buffalo.

[9] Gould, John, 1857 *Proceedings of the Zoological Society of London*: 160–162.

THOMAS COULTER (1793–1843) IN NORTH AMERICA: SOME BIBLIOGRAPHIC PROBLEMS AND SOME SOLUTIONS

E. Charles Nelson

National Botanic Gardens,
Glasnevin,
Dublin 9, Ireland

Before the image of a man as a naturalist may be sketched clearly in an historical context, or that man's particular course in history charted with even a tolerable degree of accuracy, many different "avenues" may have to be "trodden" and many questions posed. In both it is necessary to make enquiries in the places inhabited or visited by the subject of research. Thomas Coulter, an Irish student of botany, entomology, mineralogy, and other branches of the natural sciences, studied in his home country, before going to Europe and then embarking on a journey and sojourn lasting a decade in Mexico and California, whence he returned with numerous botanical specimens. However, he only published two works; one was a monograph on the Dipsacaceae and the other an account of the geography of California. His diaries, it is generally stated, were lost and few letters are recorded as surviving, so that it has not been possible to provide more than brief sketches of his travels. Yet some published narratives give details not available in Coulter's own publications, which must have been derived from unpublished sources; the elucidation of these sources presented the problems and yielded the solutions—as yet partial—of this paper.

COULTER—A BIOGRAPHICAL SUMMARY

Thomas Coulter was born on 28 September 1793[1], the eldest child of Samuel (b. 1755) and Anne (née Dickie, b. 1772) Coulter who were married on 26 December 1792. Samuel Coulter was a gentleman landowner in the Dundalk area, on the east coast of Ireland, north of Dublin. Thomas was born, almost certainly, in the family home called "Carnbeg" near Dundalk[2], and was brought up there with his brothers (Joseph, Samuel, and Robert) and his sister Jane but their parents died when the children were still very young— Samuel died in 1801 and Anne in the following year. After their parents' deaths, the children were "adopted" by Joseph Coulter, a younger brother of their father, and his wife Jane, who also eventually had six children of their own.

Thomas was educated in Dundalk at the school of the Rev. Dr Neilson and he entered the University of Dublin (Trinity College) where he studied

Contributions to the History of North American Natural History. Society for the Bibliography of Natural History, London, 1983.

mechanics, chemistry and natural science. In 1817, Thomas graduated with
the degree of Bachelor of Arts but continued his studies until he obtained
the degrees of Master of Arts and Bachelor of Medicine in 1820.[3] Afterwards
he went to Paris and spent at least part of his time studying botany at the
Jardin des Plantes. The reason for his departure from Ireland is not known,
but he may have wished to study under one of the eminent French botanists,
such as René Desfontaines. In May 1822[4] he moved to Geneva in order to
study under Augustin-Pyramus de Candolle, who was perhaps the leading
botanist in Europe, and established in Geneva where, according to Frans
Stafleu,[5] his herbarium and library formed "one of the great plant taxonomic
workshops of the world". De Candolle was embarking on his great
Prodromus at this time, and under his tutelage, Thomas Coulter prepared a
monograph on the Dipsacaceae, which was read before the Société de
Physique et d'Histoire Naturelle de Genève on 4 September 1823.[6]

Two days later,[7] Coulter left Geneva and returned to the British Isles. In
June 1824 he was residing in Soho, London, but indicated to de Candolle
that within a few months he would be departing.[8] It is said by his friend
and memorialist, the Rev. Dr Thomas Romney Robinson,[9] that Coulter
planned to travel to South America to explore the region between Buenos
Ayres and Lake Titicaca, and thence to proceed to California and either
Mexico or Canada. But, according to Robinson, Coulter was "induced" to
change his plans and was engaged as "medical attendant" by the Real del
Monte mining company which was reopening silver mines in Mexico employ-
ing British personnel including miners from Cornwall.[10]

Coulter left for Mexico on 22 September 1824[11] and spent the following
ten years there and in the region between Monterey and the River Colorado
in southern and south-eastern California—his travels in North America are
detailed below. During these years he sent living cacti from Mexico to de
Candolle in Geneva and to the Trinity College Botanic Garden in Dublin.
He returned to Europe in 1834 with a large collection of Mexican and
Californian herbarium specimens—it is estimated that his collections included
50,000 specimens, as well as about 1,000 wood samples with accompanying
herbarium vouchers.[9] He did little more than sort and arrange his herbarium
after his return; no botanical publications resulted.

Coulter's movements, following his return to Europe, are not certain. He
returned to Ireland initially, but by January 1835 he was in London; in
February and March he sent two letters on Upper California to the Royal
Geographical Society in London.[12]. He attended the meeting of the British
Association for the Advancement of Science in Dublin in August that year.
In January 1836 he was present at the first evening scientific meeting held
by the Royal Dublin Society, when he exhibited cones of *Pinus coulteri* D.
Don and *P. lambertiana* Douglas as well as "a *Thuja* and *Taxodium
sempervirens*" (= *Sequoia sempervirens* (D. Don) Endlicher), from
California, and commented on the best method of getting seeds from
California to Ireland.[13] In 1837 he obtained his doctorate in medicine from
the University of Dublin, although he never practised medicine as "a trade".

Some time before 1838, Coulter took up residence in Dublin and was given
rooms in Trinity College, where he housed his library and herbarium. At

this time the herbarium was still his property although he had suggested to the University that it should be acquired for the Botany School. The death of the Provost, Dr Lloyd, and his replacement by Dr Sadleir caused Coulter to leave the College taking his herbarium with him;[14] seemingly, his relations with the new Provost were not amicable. However, circumstances changed, and following negotiations in 1840, the University agreed to take the herbarium.

Coulter returned to Trinity College in June 1840, and presented his herbarium to the University in return for rooms, a small salary and "Commons" (meals). He was appointed curator of the herbarium on 15 June 1840[15] and vigorously set about improving not only the botanical collections but also those of the geological and zoological sections of the University museum. In July 1840 he travelled to Paris and Geneva, by way of London, on herbarium business. In 1842, the University purchased his collection of shells and, on behalf of the College, Coulter made several important purchases of collections of English and Irish insects and Phillipine shells.[16].

Coulter's health was not robust; he suffered from various illnesses in Mexico, and in Ireland, in his later years, from rheumatism and gout. In April 1843 he was caught in a rain storm in County Wicklow and was forced to walk a long distance as his party had "lost" their transport.[17] He never fully recovered from his ordeal and died in Trinity College on 26 November 1843. He was mourned by the University and accorded a dignified funeral; the College bell was tolled for five days[18] and his body was escorted from the University by all the undergradutes, Scholars, Fellows, and the Provost.[19]

During his life Coulter received various honours. In March 1819 he was elected a member of the Royal Irish Academy, Ireland's premier academic society. In December 1835, the Royal Dublin Society elected him an honorary member, "on the ground of his valuable botanical research in North America and the general addition he has made to that department of science". In 1838 he was elected an Honorary Fellow of the Royal College of Physicians of Ireland.

In 1824, Karl Kunth, in *Nova Genera et Species Plantarum*,[20] described a genus in the Leguminosae which he named after Coulter—*Coulteria*: Genus dictum in honorem Thomasii Coulteri, praeclari Hiberniae botanici, qui de Dipsacearum familia egregium edidit commentarium, nunc autem, nobili botanices studio excitatus, ad Regnum Chilense accuratius explorandum accingit sese". In 1845, his successor as curator of the Trinity College herbarium, William Henry Harvey[21], described a number of Californian plants based on Coulter's collections, including the beautiful white poppy, the matilija, *Romneya coulteri*—the generic name commemorates Thomas Coulter's friend, the Irish astronomer, Romney Robinson. Many other plants bear the specific epithet *coulteri* in his honour; some are listed by Coville.[22]

COULTER—BIBLIOGRAPHIC PROBLEMS OF HIS AMERICAN WORK

It is not my intention to document in detail Coulter's travels and work in this paper, rather I wish to list the unpublished sources available, to point out some problems, and relate some solutions which have recently come about.

The earliest biography is that of Romney Robinson[9] which was used by later authors including D'Alton and O'Flanagan[23], Coville[22], Wright[24], and Coats[10]. A list of biographical sources is available in F. A. Stafleu and R. S. Cowan's *Taxonomic Literature II*, (vol. 1; 1976). In this present account I wish to concentrate on manuscript sources.

As stated, Coulter published no autobiography or journal of his travels. According to Robinson[9], "a case of [Coulter's] botanical manuscripts, and the material of a personal narrative, disappeared, and could never be traced... in the transport from London to Dublin", shortly after Coulter returned to Europe in 1834. While this is the generally repeated account, Coulter himself makes no reference in letters to the loss of manuscripts; his only remarks relate to the use of his journals to document his dated but unlocalized and unnamed herbarium specimens (see letter XIII in Appendix). Two years after Coulter's death, William Hooker attempted to persuade William Harvey to do some concerted taxonomic work on Coulter's herbarium and enquired about journals. In an unpublished letter[25], Harvey told Hooker that he had been informed by Thomas Fleming Bergin "that the whole of [Coulter's journals], together with some other valuable manuscripts were lost on his return voyage from Mexico. They were packed in a box by themselves, and all the boxes arrived safely except this one." Two years later, Harvey told Hooker again[26] that he had "no record of Coulter's progress and none now exists. The journals as I have often been told by his friends, were all lost in a box, that was abstracted from his baggage, which was supposed to contain some matters that might be inconvenient to parties connected with the mines. However this be, the journals are not forthcoming... ". This latter explanation is not unreasonable, given Coulter's managerial role in the rich silver mines. The question which may be posed is whether his journals still survive in mining archives in Mexico. The loss of these manuscripts, as Harvey remarked[25], is "much to be regretted, as they were doubtless (to judge by [Coulter's] viva-voce travels) most amusing and valuable". Their recovery would be an event of considerable interest.

However, it is clear from the correspondence of Frederick Coville, of the United States Department of Agriculture, and Joseph Coulter, a nephew of Thomas, that a journal relating to the period 18 August 1824 to 11 October 1827 was extant in 1896; it was noted by Wright[24] who stated that Joseph Coulter had "several of his uncle's note-books... mostly filled with observations for Lat. and Long. made when in South [*sic*] America." According to the Coulter-Coville correspondence, Joseph Coulter sent this manuscript journal to Coville at the Smithsonian Institute, Washington, and informed Coville that "if you desire to retain it I shall not object... "[27] —Coville did so. This manuscript was studied by Roger McVaugh in 1943 and was partly transcribed by him in a paper detailing Coulter's first three years in Mexico.[11] The manuscript is in the Smithsonian Archives, but I have not yet had the opportunity to study it.[28]

Coville did not have this journal, nor did he use the letters which Thomas Coulter had written to Augustin-Pyramus de Candolle and his son Alphonse, when he compiled his account of Coulter's travels;[22] the letters were known to Coville who stated that he had "recently had access" to them and that they "may hereafter be incorporated into a more detailed account of Coulter's labors". Coville did not publish any further papers on Coulter and the Coulter-de Candolle correspondence is still unpublished. I have studied the de Candolle letters and they are included in the appended catalogue.

The most complete account of Coulter's American years was published in 1969 by Alice Coats in her book *The Quest for Plants*.[10] Probably due to restrictions imposed by her publishers, Miss Coats gave only a very general bibliography and did not cite in detail the many unpublished sources which she clearly consulted. In respect to Thomas Coulter's journeys, a careful examination of Miss Coats's narrative, and those published previously, showed that she had had access to information and details not known to earlier authors, but her only acknowledgement was to "Mrs H. Harrison, a collateral descendent of Thomas Coulter, for her obliging loan of family letters and papers". Miss Coats died in 1978 and despite numerous enquiries of her colleagues and acquaintances, no-one could help the present author to contact Mrs Harrison. In December 1981, I placed a letter seeking help in the *Dundalk Democrat* newspaper, hoping that some person in the Dundalk region might be able to assist in tracing Thomas Coulter's relatives—the result was most gratifying and this paper was made possible. Through various members of the Coulter family, especially Brian Coulter, I have been allowed access to all manuscripts in their possession. An examination of these shows that they are the letters and papers seen and used by Miss Coats. However it is clear that Miss Coats obtained background information on Mexican mines and some other details of Coulter's work from another source, not as yet identified by the present author.

It should be noted that Miss Coats did not study the correspondence between Coulter and the de Candolles; this includes two valuable additional letters addressed from Petic (now Hermosilla) in Mexico and from the confluence of the Colorado and Gila rivers on the border of California and Arizona (near the modern town Yuma).

The following annotated table of places and dates associated with Coulter's travels is based on the publications of Couter,[12] Douglas,[29] Coville,[22] McVaugh,[11] and Coats,[10] as well as the letters listed in the Appendix (cited by the Roman numeral of their catalogue number).

18 August 1824	—London (first entry in journal—see McVaugh)
22 September 1824	—depart London (McVaugh)
13 or 14 October 1824	—arrive Funchal, Madeira (McVaugh)
5 November 1824	—depart Funchal (McVaugh)
8 December 1824	—arrive Port Maria, Jamaica (McVaugh; see also letter VI)
6 January 1825	—depart Kingston, Jamaica (McVaugh)
27 January 1825	—arrive at Vera Cruz, Mexico (McVaugh, Coats)
	—travel via Xalapa, Apam, Tlalayote, Tualancingo (McVaugh)
25 February 1825	—arrive Real del Monte (McVaugh, Coats)

16 April 1825	—left for short visit to Mexico City (17–27 April) (McVaugh)
29 April 1825	—returned to Real del Monte (McVaugh)
17 June 1825	—left for short visit (2nd.) to Mexico City (McVaugh)
28 June 1825	—returned to Real del Monte (McVaugh)
6 August 1825	—Real del Monte (letter to his sister; IV)
31 October 1825	—depart Real del Monte (McVaugh)
	—travel via Pachuca, Tepetango, San Juan del Rio, Queretaro, Celaya, Salamanca, Guanajuato, Silao, Leon, Lagos, Aguas, Calientes (McVaugh)
21 November 1825	—arrive at Veta Grande mine near Zacatecas (McVaugh; see also letter V)
12 December 1825	—left for a hurried trip to Bolanos (14–26 December) (McVaugh, Coats)
30 December 1825	—returned to Veta Grande (McVaugh)
December 1825—January 1826	—made meteorological observations at Zactecas (Coulter)
26 May 1826	—Zacatecas (letter to his sister; V)
8 September 1826	—Zacatecas (letter to de Candolle; VI)
15 January 1827	—depart Zacatecas (McVaugh)
2 February 1827	—arrive Zimapan (McVaugh)
April 1827	—Zimapan—meteorological observations (Coulter)
21 August 1827	—Zimapan (letter to his sister; VII)
11 October 1827	—Zimapan (last entry in journal—see McVaugh)
(? Spring) 1828	—sent cacti to Geneva and Dublin
(? August) 1828	—contract expired, not renewed
December 1828	—revolution in Mexico (see letter XII)
12 December 1829	—San Jose "a few leagues from Pitis [sic]" (Coulter)
December 1829	—Petic, Sonora Alta (Coulter)
20 December 1830	—Petic (letter to de Candolle; VIII)
12 August 1831	—Guaymas (letter to his sister; IX)
13 or 14 August 1831	—departs Guaymas for Monterey on an American brig (see letter IX)
(late September or early October 1831)	—arrives in Monterey, California (see letter X)
October 1831	—travels via Santa Barbara to San Gabriel (see letter X)
20 October 1831	—Santa Barbara (Bancroft Library ms.)
3 November 1831	—San Gabriel (letter to his sister; X)
23 November 1831	—Monterey (Douglas)
22 January—20 March 1832	—Monterey—chronometer readings (Coulter)
6 April 1832	—Santa Barbara (Coulter)
23 April 1832	—San Gabriel (Coulter)
30 April 1832	—La Pala (Coulter)

8 May 1832	—Ford on Colorado River (Coulter)
16 May 1832	—Ford on Colorado River (letter to de Candolle; XI)
17 May 1832	—begins return journey to Monterey (Coulter; see also letter XI)
27 May 1832	—La Pala (Coulter)
15 June 1832	—San Gabriel (Coulter)
5–7 July 1832	—Santa Barbara (Coulter)
19 July 1832	—Monterey (Coulter)
? 1832	—returned to Mexico by sea, via San Diego (letter to Hartnell; XII)
9 April 1833	—Guanajuato (Bancroft Library ms.)
27 April 1833	—Mexico City (letter to Hartnell; XII)
4 November 1833	—Guanajuato (letter to his sister; XIII)
	—returned to British Isles (see letter XIV)
9 January 1835	—London (letter to de Candolle; XIV)

CONCLUSION

The problem of identifying the sources used by Alice Coats is mostly solved, although work is continuing on the remaining unidentified sources. Other manuscripts and letters relating to Thomas Coulter may exist; for example, letters to the English botanist Aylmer Bourke Lambert are noted by Robinson[9] but these cannot be located and are not among the known collections of Lambert's correspondence. Attempts are now being made to find Coulter's correspondence with his close friend Romney Robinson. Studies are in progress in Dublin, mainly in Trinity College, on Coulter's work there, and it is hoped to incorporate the results of these researches into a more detailed biography of Thomas Coulter.

Initially, I was pessimistic about the prospect of tracing Alice Coats's sources, however with the co-operation of several people, especially Brian A. Coulter (Belfast, Northern Ireland), C. T. McCrea (Blackrock, County Louth, Eire), Mr and Mrs P. Harrison (Sutton Coldfield, England) and Dr M. O. Coulter (Tiverton, England), as well as librarians and archivists in Berkeley, Pittsburgh, Washington (United States), Kew, and the Royal Geographical Society, London, Geneva, and Trinity College, Dublin, much new material has been found which will allow the construction of a fuller study of Thomas Coulter.

Romney Robinson[9] described his friend as "a noble and commanding person" and considered that Coulter was an heroic martyr to science. In his panegyric, Robinson wrote:

> The Present ere long becomes the Past;... the stream of time in its flow washes all that is earthly from the ruin, and leaves in imperishable brightness the grains of gold and gem which it contained, the treasures of the Future.

Those treasures include the manuscripts and publications of such people as Thomas Coulter, "grains of gold and gem" scattered throughout the world, but fortunately preserved for our study.[30]

NOTES AND REFERENCES

[1] Biographical information and information about the Coulter family are derived from manuscripts in the possession of B. A. Coulter and P. Harrison.

[2] According to *Alumni Dublinensis* (G. D. Burtchaell and T. V. Sadleir, eds. 1935, edition 2.), Coulter was born in London. However the original manuscript register indicates that he was born in County Louth (i.e. Dundalk). The mistake in *Alumni* probably arose because the county's name is contracted to "Lou.", misinterpreted "Lon." (i.e. London).

[3] *Alumni Dublinensis*, op. cit.

[4] see letter I (listed in Appendix).

[5] F. A. Stafleu, 1966 The great *Prodromus* (reprinted in *Adanson, Labillarière and de Candolle*, 1967). Lehre.

[6] T. Coulter, 1823 *Mémoire sur les Dispsacées*. Genève.

[7] see letter II (listed in Appendix).

[8] see letter III (listed in Appendix).

[9] T. R. Robinson, 1844 (Obituary of Thomas Coulter) in *Proceedings of the Royal Irish Academy* 2: 553–557.

[10] A. M. Coats, 1969 *The quest for plants*. pp. 341–344. London. (This book was published in the United States under the title *The Plant Hunters*.)

[11] R. McVaugh, 1943 The travels of Thomas Coulter, 1824–1827. *Journal of the Washington Academy of Sciences* 33: 65–70. A photostat copy of the original journal is being supplied to the author and will be deposited in the archives of Trinity College, Dublin, on the completion of this research, along with copies of all other manuscripts studied.

[12] T. Coulter, 1835 Notes on Upper California. *Journal of the Royal Geographical Society of London* 5: 59–70. This paper is an edited version of two letters sent to A. Maconochie of the Royal Geographical Society; substantial sections of both letters have been omitted. The letters, dated 11 February 1835 and 23 March 1835, are preserved in the archives of the Society; they are not included in the appended catalogue. I have studied photostat copies.

[13] (Report of the evening scientific meeting, 26 January 1836). *Proceedings of the Royal Dublin Society* 73. (1835–1836).

[14] see letter XVI (listed in Appendix).

[15] see letters XVII, XIX (listed in Appendix).

[16] see letters XIX–XXI, XXIV (listed in Appendix).

[17] see letters XXV, XXVI (listed in Appendix).

[18] Trinity College, Dublin, Muniments; Bursar's vouchers P4/238/80.

[19] Details are in unlisted items among manuscripts in possession of B. A. Coulter.

[20] A. de Humboldt, A. Bonpland and C. S. Kunth, 1815(–1825) *Nova genera et species plantarum*. vol. 6 p. 328 (1824). Paris.

[21] W. H. Harvey, 1845 Description of a new genus of Papaveraceae, detected by the late Dr. Coulter in California. *London Journal of Botany* 4: 73–76.

[22] F. V. Coville, 1895 The botanical explorations of Thomas Coulter in Mexico and California. *Botanical Gazette* 20: 519–531.

[23] J. D'Alton and J. R. O'Flanagan, 1864 *The history of Dundalk and its environs*. pp. 346–351. Dundalk.

[24] E. P. Wright, 1896 in *Notes from the Botany School, Dublin* 1: 3–4.

[25] Hooker Correspondence, Royal Botanic Gardens, Kew; English letters, vol. 23, no. 45.

[26] Hooker Correspondence, Royal Botanic Gardens, Kew; English letters, vol. 27, no. 245.

[27] This letter was found by me, quite by accident, in the General Autograph Collection of the Hunt Institute for Botanical Documentation, Carnegie-Mellon University, Pittsburgh. Coville's letters to J. A. Coulter are in the possession of B. A. Coulter.

[28] The manuscript was traced by Mrs Ruth Schallert in March 1982; see note 11.

[29] Douglas's letter to W. J. Hooker, from Monterey, Upper California, dated 23 November 1831, was published in a heavily edited version in *Companion to the Botanical Magazine* 2: 149–151 (1836). the full unedited text (based on a transcript in the Provincial Library, Victoria,

British Columbia of the original manuscript preserved in Kew) was published in the *California Historical Society Quarterly* 2*(3)* in 1923, and is dated 20 November 1831. I have not been able to examine the original manuscript to resolve this confusion.

[30] A portrait in oils of Thomas Coulter is in Trinity College, Dublin. It was presented to the University in 1963 by Miss Barbara Coulter (now Mrs B. Hannah) and her brother, Dr Michael Coulter. It is reproduced in: A. M. Coats, 1964 Thomas Coulter and Romney Robinson *Gardeners Chronicle* **156**: 102 (25 July). A. M. Coats, 1965. Notes on some portraits of British botanists and gardeners. *Huntia* **2**: 192–193 (in this paper Coulter's year of death is incorrectly given as 1846). E. C. Nelson, 1982. An Irishman in the country of flowers. *Zoonooz* 55*(3)*: 16–18.

APPENDIX

Chronological list of letters written by Thomas Coulter

Those cited as "Coulter Mss" are in the possession of B. A. Coulter, but photostat copies will be deposited in the archives of the National Botanic Gardens, Dublin, and in the Library, Trinity College, Dublin.

The addresses are those given on the letters; information added by this author is enclosed in square brackets. All letters are in English unless indicated.

I   Place Maurice N.º 20, Geneva, [Switzerland]; 22 May 1822; to **Mrs [Jane] Davison** [née Coulter, sister of Thomas], Dundalk, Ireland.
Had been 2 weeks in Geneva; mentions desire to study under de Candolle; had letter of introduction from Robert Brown; environs of Geneva; his personal feelings; family matters.
Coulter Mss.

II   Geneva; 28 July 1823; to **Mrs [Jane] Davison**, Dundalk, Ireland.
Tour in Savoy with de Candolle and others; family matters; personal finances; intends leaving Geneva on 6 September; returning *via* Paris and maybe Strasbourg.
Coulter Mss.

III   21 A Frith Street, Soho, London; le 5 Juin 1824; to [**Augustin-Pyramus de Candolle**, Geneva].
(*In French*) Introduces Mr Nimmo from Ireland; his own situation; expects to leave in August or beginning of September; a manuscript on Dipsacaceae not yet ready; *Prodromus*.
Gray Herbarium, Cambridge, Mass., U.S.A.

IV   Mineral de Monte, Mexico; 6 August 1825; to **Rev. David Davison** [brother-in-law], care of Mr Vincent, No. 2, Upper Georges Place, St John St. Road, London.
Complains that only Davison has written since he left England; family matters; does not expect to return home for "five or six years"; his herbarium in Ireland; Mexican climate.
Coulter Mss.

V   Veta Grande, Zacatecas, [Mexico]; 28 May 1826; to **Mrs [Jane] Davison**, care of John Taylor Esqre, London (endorsed "Not known at Mr John Taylors at 7 or 65 Tower Street Wm Piggott.")

Has been six months in Zacatecas; "I am well and busy", family matters; society in Mexico; violence in Zacatecas; botany makes "but little progress"; instructions concerning his herbarium.
Coulter Mss.

VI Zacatecas; 8 September 1826; to **Mons.ʳ Le Prof.ʳ. [Augustin-Pyramus] De Candolle**, Genève, Suisse.
(*In French*) Comments on Humbolt's description of Mexico; violence in Zacatecas; voyage from England and companions; service to mining company in Zacatecas; details of the mines; few plants to collect; will change his mind about Chile; mentions California; mentions Kunth's publication of *Coulteria*; would have preferred de Candolle to have honoured him thus; personal matters.
A-P. de Candolle Mss, Conservatoire Botanique, Geneva.

VII Zimapan, [Mexico]; 21 August 1827; to **Mrs [Jane] Davison**, 18 King Square, Goswell Road, London.
Changes in company management; his own prospects not much affected but advancement unlikely; family matters; climate of Zimapan pleasant; plants plentiful; jokes of family affairs.
Coulter Mss.

VIII Petic in Sonora Alta, [Mexico]; 20 December 1830; to **Mons.ʳ Alphonse de Candolle**, Genève, Suisse.
Mentions receipt of letter from de Candolle; pleased about cacti; resigned from mines; hopes to get contract for mint; if successful will return to Europe and visit Geneva; seen no books but those sent by Alphonse's father; will travel north to California if mint contract not granted.
Alphonse de Candolle Mss, Conservatoire Botanique, Geneva.

IX Guaymas, [Mexico]; 12 August 1831; to **Mrs [Jane] Davison**, Rosoman House, Islington, London.
Resigned mint contract and withdrawn from other "motives"; health suffering; returning to botany; leaving "tomorrow or next day" for Monterey by sea; feels lonely and anxious; will spend two more years and then return home; family queries; P.S. sending herbarium specimens.
Coulter Mss.

X San Gabriel in High California; 3 November 1831; to **"my dear sister"** [**Mrs Jane Davison**] but addressed to Revd David Davison, Rosoman House, Islington, London.
Been in California one month but no botanizing possible; travelled overland from Monterey; describes road and journey; family matters are depressing him; health improved due to cooler climate; local people and missions; family matters.
Coulter Mss.

XI At the ford of the River Colorado 8 miles south west of the junction of the Gila with it, [California-Arizona border]; 16 May 1832; to **Mons.ʳ Alphonse De Candolle**, Geneve, Suisse.
Tried to write in French but is "rusty"; travels in California; David Douglas; collections poor and small; "This is truly the Kingdom of Desolation"; geography of California and botanical prospects; "on the whole the flora

is... but poor in numbers; some species very strange; will stay another year.
Alphonse de Candolle Mss, Conservatoire Botanique, Geneva.

XII   Mexico [City]; Saturday 27 April 1833; to **William E. Hartnell**,
Monterey in California.
Encloses circular on his new enterprise about to start in Guanajuato; details
of recent events in Mexican mines; situation in California; "That the
copperskins must melt before the whites, in time, is a most melancholy
certainty"; his health since leaving San Diego; mentions two priests.
H. H. Bancroft Collection, Vallejo Collection, document 11 (C–B 31),
University of California, Berkeley.

XIII   Guanaxuato, Mexico; 4 November 1833; to **Mrs [Jane] Davison**,
Rosoman House, Islington, London.
Had no letter for a long time; cholera in city so he must act as doctor though
he had never done this "as a trade" before; revolution just ended; describes
bombardment and his reactions; his affairs since December 1828 when he
was in business making alum; returned to this, but new revolution "put
back" prospects; "really I don't like to be always poor"; family matters.
Coulter Mss.

XIV   Rosoman House, Islington, London; 9 January 1835; to **Mons! Le
Prof! [Augustin-Pyramus] De Candolle**, Genève, Suisse.
(*In French*) Mentions having been in Ireland; thanks for offer of use of
herbarium and library but must stay in London for present; had begun to
write "history of my journey"; arranging plants which "are all in order of
collection" and without any other mark except the date which corresponds
to my journals"; comments on London society; intends going to British
Association in Dublin in August.
A–P. de Candolle Mss, Conservatoire Botaniuqe, Geneva.

XV   Rosoman House, Islington, London; 27 March 1835; to **Dr [William]
Hooker**, Glasgow, Scotland.
Will be pleased to exchange plants once sorted; was unable to visit Santa Fe
region; David Douglas; would be pleased to visit Scotland; health "broken";
hopes to meet at British Association in Dublin.
Hooker Correspondence, South American Letters 1832–1837, vol. LXVII,
ms. 17; Royal Botanic Gardens, Kew, London.

XVI   Myrtle Lodge, Kingstown (near Dublin), [Dun Laoghaire, Ireland]; 20
April 1838; to **Mrs [Jane] Davison**, 3 Euston Square, London.
Family matters; own affairs; must vacate house and college rooms; new
Provost of University unlike predecessor; health better.
Coulter Mss.

XVII   40 [Trinity] College, Dublin; 5 June 1840; to **Robert Coulter** [his
brother], Dundalk.
Just "passed the agony" of moving into college his herbarium and library;
his health.
Coulter Mss.

XVIII   40 [Trinity] College, [Dublin]; 28 June 1840; to **Robert Coulter**,
Dundalk.

Reports successful conclusion of negotiations with University; will pay "flying" visit to Dundalk soon.
Coulter Mss.

XIX   40 [Trinity] College, Dublin; 8 July 1840; to **Robert Coulter**, Dundalk.
Unable to visit Dundalk as he must travel to London, Paris, and Geneva; hopes to go to British Association in Glasgow in September; finances; P.S. (dated 9 July) details of terms agreed with University for possession of his herbarium.
Coulter Mss.

XX   3 Euston Square, London; 23 July 1840; to **[Dr William Hooker**, Glasgow].
On way to Paris and Geneva; will exchange duplicates but herbarium now belongs to University; Mexican and Californian plants ready within one year; pines seen by Don; none brought home alive only unripe cones; collection of shells; will meet James Mackay curator of Trinity College Botanic Garden in Edinburgh and accompany him to Glasgow.
Hooker Correspondence, English Letters 1840 (A–H), vol XIV, ms 103; Royal Botanic Gardens, Kew, London.

XXI   40 [Trinity] College, Dublin; 26 January 1842; to **Mrs [Jane] Davison**, 499 Rauische Strasse, Halle, Prussia.
Family matters; his work in college museums; his health; purchase of Philippine shells and English insects [see XXIII below]; has added 4000 species to herbarium; preparing himself to lecture in botany "if called for"; local elections.
Coulter Mss.

XXII   40 [Trinity] College, Dublin; 22 August 1842; to **Mrs [Jane] Davison**, 499 Rauische Strasse, Halle, Prussia.
Family questions and affairs; own health for past years; his feelings when he was near death some years previously.
Coulter Mss.

XXIII   40 [Trinity] College, Dublin; 1 November 1842; to **John Thomas Dickie** [his uncle], Clonaleenan, Dundalk.
Concerning Joseph Dickie; recounts his own attempts to join a rifle club [—the letter is accompanied by diagrams of targets including one shot on 6 October 1842 by Coulter "the best ever made" in Ireland.]
Coulter Mss.

XXIV   40 [Trinity] College; 11 January 1843; to **Revd Dr MacDonnell**, Bursar's Office, [Trinity College, Dublin].
Encloses accounts for expenditure on herbarium and museum; notes purchase of Cuming's Philippine shells (487 specimens) for £100; Curtis's British insects (7,656 specimens) £162.2.0.; Tardy's Irish insects (about 10,000 specimens) £160.14.6.; these collections and his own shells unequalled in Ireland; has 4,615 extra-European and 4,500 European specimens "in good working order" in herbarium; rearranging them according to Endlicher.
Trinity College Muniments, Bursar's vouchers P4/234/23a, Manuscript Dept, Library, Trinity College, Dublin.

XXV   40 [Trinity] College; Dublin; 11 September 1843; to **Mrs [Jane] Davidson**, Heidelberg.
Health poor due to being caught in rain in County Wicklow; has rheumatism; hopes to travel to Dundalk in following week; had attack of gout "short, but oh how sweet"; family affairs and ancestry.
Coutler Mss.

XXVI   40 [Trinity] College, Dublin; 15 November 1843; to **Revd David Davison**, Library, Red Cross Street, London.
Although not stated explicity Coulter feels he may die soon; his health is very poor; asks that this be kept from Jane but that she should know he is not well; answers query about an antiquarian society in Dublin; obscure reference to "papers"; will write shortly to Jane. [Thomas Coulter died on 26 November 1843].
Coulter Mss.

BIBLIOGRAPHY AND NATURAL HISTORY NEW SOURCES FOR THE CONTRIBUTIONS OF THE AMERICAN NATURALIST, TITIAN RAMSAY PEALE

Charlotte M. Porter
Assistant Curator
The Florida State Museum,
University of Florida, Gainesville,
Florida 32611

Bibliography, however defined, has long played a central role within the study of natural history. This traditional association of bibliography and natural history not only parallels the obvious dependence of scientific discovery of plants and animals upon publication, but also reflects an older idea of all Creation as a Book of Nature. Despite the absence of any heuristic value, this rather humble approach to Nature as a book, whose pages are open to all, has remained one of the most successful and certainly one of the most attractive ideas in the history of western science.[1] Needless to say, the inherent democratic values were so appealing that Charles Willson Peale (1742–1827) chose the Book of Nature as the symbol for the first true museum opened to the American public in 1786.[2]

Even as our understanding of both the natural world and scientific ideas becomes increasingly complex, not infrequently, the results of routine bibliographic inquiries can surprisingly challenge entrenched evaluations of earlier scientific periods. Elsewhere, I have discussed two related examples of new insights revealed by a straight-forward bibliographic approach to natural history books published by members of the Philadelphia Academy of Natural Sciences following the War of 1812.[3] In the first case, examination of these works showed a self-conscious program of publication, the purpose of which was to emulate the success of Alexander Wilson's *American Ornithology* (1808–1814) in other areas of natural history.[4] Thomas Say, George Ord, Charles Lucien Bonaparte, John Godman, and Thomas Nuttall all attempted to complete similar, grandly conceived books describing American insects, birds, mammals, and plants. In addition to their texts, their personal correspondence, the Academy's papers, and the accompanying popular press attest to their highly unified purpose and distinctive approach to American natural history, unexpected from such a young scientific organization.[5] Indeed, the Academy approach proved to be so organized that an equally important group of publications, often by these same authors, was discouraged, and, in some cases, actually suppressed by the scientific community at large.[6] Works by Say, Constantine Rafinesque, and Titian Ramsay Peale remained unpublished in the format they merited and hence, for the large part, remained unknown to their contemporaries.[7]

Contributions to the History of North American Natural History. Society for the Bibliography of Natural History, London, 1983.

In this regard, two manuscript groups are especially helpful in reviewing the controversial lifework of the American naturalist, Titian Ramsay Peale, almost one hundred years after his death. These are the 283 newly acquired drawings by Titian Peale at the American Philosophical Society and the massive sea journal of William L. Hudson (1794–1862) at the American Museum of Natural History in New York City.[8] Hudson was second in command of the Wilkes Expedition (1838–1842) and Captain of the U.S.S. *Peacock,* the ship on which Peale sailed with the expedition until 1841, when she wrecked in the mouth of the Columbia River. Ironically, having survived this calamity, part of the Hudson Journal was lost in private hands during the 1950s and now apparently exists only in photocopy.[9] Peale's records did not fare as well. He wrote to his brother Franklin: "Next morning not a vestage [*sic*] of the ship remained, all our collections (the most valuable of any obtained) all my knick-knacks, clothes—everything but my rifle and the clothes on my back were—gone—".[10] Sadly, more of Titian's work was lost to historians with the dispersal of the Peale family museum collection in 1846.[11]

Titian Peale's life literally spanned the nineteenth century. Son of Charles Willson Peale, the polymathic proprietor of the Philadelphia Museum, Titian was born in Philosophical Hall in 1799 and died in Washington, D.C., in 1885. At the precocious age of eighteen, the self-styled "Dr T. R. Peale" of Girard Street finished a slim portfolio of watercolour drawings for Thomas Say to use in the first illustrated insect book to be published in this country.[12] The American Philosophical Society owns the elegant watercolors and now can boast young Peale's annotated sketchbook for the same year (1817) showing the caterpillars he raised and the plants on which they fed.[13] Through his long association with the Philadelphia Academy of Natural Sciences, Titian helped assemble American collections which gave reality to the Linnaean system of classification, and in turn, to the new French or "natural systems," and finally, to the irrefutable impact of British natural history culminating in Darwinism.[14]

The Hudson Journal and the new drawings certainly contain biographical information. However, because they will only add footnotes to the already excellent biography of Titian Peale by Jessie Poesch and the extensive Peale Family Papers edited by Lillian Miller,[15] these manuscripts will be viewed here with an eye to the public reception of Titian Peale's scientific endeavor. The recently acquired drawings double the holdings of Titian Peale at the American Philosophical Society. Besides the entomological studies already mentioned, the new group includes Titian's scientific drawings for two major exploring expeditions: the Stephen Long Expedition (1819–1820), a topographical mission to the Rocky Mountains, and the politically complex, U.S. Exploring Expedition under Lt Charles Wilkes, which charted parts of Antarctica and innumerable Pacific islands from Australia to Hawaii.[16]

Titian Peale's claims to scientific recognition beyond his standing as an illustrator rested upon these expeditions. His father, Charles Willson Peale, was to have illustrated a natural history of the earlier Lewis and Clark Expedition (1804–1806), but too many of the specimens arrived in Philadelphia too poorly preserved for accurate presentation.[17] Consequently, the next government expedition to the trans-Mississippi West took along the best specialists the nation could provide. Titian Peale, age twenty, a skilled marksman, draftsman, and conservator, was appointed assistant to the official zoologist, Thomas Say, age thirty-two. During the second season, they were joined by a twenty-two year old botanist from New York State named Edwin James. Back at the Philadelphia Academy, the birds Titian collected were systematically described by a visiting ornithologist, Charles Lucien Bonaparte, age twenty-two, and James's plant collections were written up by the country's leading botanist, John Torrey, twenty-nine.[18] The youth of these naturalists is noteworthy, for it lent a definite character to the period's natural history books. Literally thousands of species were boldly declared to be new in brightly colored plates and inadequately researched descriptions.

Their youth also lent something of a rough-and-ready quality to exhibits at the Peale Museum. The eccentric British naturalist and traveller, Charles Waterton, quite rightly complained about the cumulative, ghoulish effects of mounting mammals with open jaws.[19] Certainly, Titian's western drawings do show bobcats and wolves baring their characteristic dentition, and his watercolor of a prairie wolf devouring the head of a mule deer is, perhaps, the only documented visualization of a Peale Museum display we have. Edwin James provided the humorous explanation for this roundabout method of exhibiting not the coyote, but the mule deer! The dried skin of the mule or black-tailed deer sent back by the Long party from Arkansas was "so much injured by depredating insects, that it has not been judged proper to mount it entire. The head has therefore been separated from the remaining portion of the skin, and may be seen in the Philadelphia Museum, placed under the foot of a prairie wolf."[20]

James's published narrative of the expedition included a catalogue of mammals by Thomas Say. Many of Peale's field sketches and the finished drawings which were never published correspond to entries in Say's catalogue and depict animals that were first seen by Lewis and Clark fifteen years earlier.[21] However, the wealth of ingeniously mounted specimens and the new western collections deposited at the Peale Museum did foster a number of illustrated publications, including John Godman's three volume work, *American Natural History*.[22]

Godman (1794–1830), who taught at the Philadelphia Anatomical Rooms, soon married Angelica Peale, Titian's niece. Because of his close relationship with the Peales, illustrations for Godman's publication of 1826 are thought to be drawn from Museum mounts.[23] Godman certainly acknowledged Titian's contributions throughout his text.[24] We now can see that several plates drawn by Charles Alexandre LeSueur are extremely close to Titian's western field drawings—namely, LeSueur's plates of the grizzly bear and the barking wolf.[25] LeSueur and Titian Peale were colleagues, and after 1817, the fellow artist-naturalists worked together closely on a number of engravings published in the Academy's *Journal*.[26] Indeed, Peale's western field drawings completed in Philadelphia in 1821 or 1822 may equally show the influence of LeSueur's more accomplished hand.

In addition to the generous illustrations, a remarkable aspect of Godman's volumes was the charming descriptions of animal behavior. Like Charles Willson Peale and Alexander Wilson, Godman was interested in the modification of animal instincts and the disarming capacity for gentleness observed among wild species. He described at length the "extreme tenderness" shown by the playful otter for her young and recorded a young fox brought to the Museum with its unexpected foster mother, a common cat![27] Godman's writings were popular in the Philadelphia area, for his volumes were the *only* comprehensive source for illustrated American mammals published in this country. Spurred by his premature death in 1830, subsequent editions made the book even more widely available.[28] A crude version of the grizzly bear plate was illustrated in Davy Crockett's *Allmanac* for 1837, and somewhat wooden copies of the wolf and bear appear rather surprisingly in Edward Hick's paintings of The Peaceable Kingdom dated 1833, 1844, and 1849.[29] Although Hicks (1780–1849) painted over sixty versions of The Peaceable Kingdom, the bear and the wolf are the only New World species shown in these masterpieces of American folk painting, which invariably include a stout child leading a lion amongst an unlikely cluster of biblical animals.[30] Hick's acknowledged source for his treatment of The Peaceable Kingdom was the well-known prophecy in Isaiah XI, verse six:

> The wolf also shall dwell with the lamb, and the leopard shall lie down with the kid; and the calf and the young lion and the fatling together; and a little child shall lead them.

By the 1830s, Hicks began to include as well identifiably American versions of those animals mentioned in the next verse:

> And the cow and the bear shall feed; their young ones shall lie down together: and the lion shall eat straw like the ox.[31]

Edward Hicks's natural history sources require more clarification. However, simple, visual comparison shows that sometime after the first edition of Godman's book, Hicks had access to those illustrations based upon Titian Peale's western drawings.[32] Certainly, Hicks, a devout Quaker, would have been attracted to those passages which described the fox living peaceably with the cat. In fact, the fox is illustrated in Godman's book on the same plate with the wolf, which I suggest is curled up with the lamb in Hicks's Peaceable Kingdom of 1844. There are additional reasons to believe that Hicks found sources for his peaceable vision in the natural history associated with the Peale Museum.[33] The decorative frame of his 1825 painting of The Falls of Niagara is inscribed with verses from "The Foresters," a poem by the ornithologist, Alexander Wilson.[34] As is well documented, Wilson based his scientific career around the Peale Museum, and his work served as Godman's model. Although it has not stood the test of time, Wilson's "Foresters" was the best read nature poem of the period, and without a doubt, brought general readers to his own and other natural history books. Hicks certainly read the poem at home in Newtown, Pennsylvania, where it was reprinted,[35] and it well may have come to his attention again through the press accompanying George Ord's 1824 edition of Wilson's work the year before Hicks undertook his Niagara composition.

Of course, it is perfectly possible that Hicks, at one time an itinerant
carriage painter who settled down in Bucks County, actually visited Peale's
Museum in nearby Philadelphia. There he would have seen the mounted
specimens discussed by Godman, and there, too, he might also have seen the
other exotic felines which inhabited his Peaceable Kingdoms.[36] Indeed, old
Peale himself was famous for using his innumerable young children to feed
and lead the wild animals living in the Museum's menagerie.[37] Lastly, the
seeds of Utopianism which found visual expression in Hicks's paintings were
already present in the Philadelphia scientific community. [See Ian MacPhail's
paper in this volume.] When the British socialist, Robert Owen came to the
United States to found a Utopian community at New Harmony, an idea
which received much publicity in the American press, he recruited at the
Philadelphia Academy of Natural Sciences in 1824.[38] Titian Peale, LeSueur,
and Godman were all members of the Academy, and several naturalists,
including LeSueur and Say, joined up with Owen and moved to New
Harmony in 1826. Equally important, the Academy's president and great
philanthropist of science, William Maclure also joined Owen's project.[39]
Maclure was a Quaker sympathizer of vast wealth who published his opinions
in inexpensive tracts. It is hard to believe that Hicks with his particular
religious concerns was either ignorant of or uninfluenced by these unusual
developments in the community around him.

The scientific influence of Philadelphia naturalists was also felt at the
national level, and during the early 1830s, members of the Academy and the
American Philosophical Society were requested by the federal government to
draw up recommendations for the country's first naval effort with scientific
aims.[40] Titian Peale served on one of the consulting committees for the U.S.
Exploring Expedition, and in 1838, sailed from Norfolk, Virginia, as the
expedition's official zoologist. On the ship *Peacock*, Peale drew various
South American ports the squadron visited *en route* to the Pacific and the
great ice islands on a side trip to Antarctica. Characteristically, Peale was
the only member of the scientific corps to volunteer for that daring venture
into uncharted waters.[41] Once in the Pacific Ocean, Peale made prolific
studies of seabirds, fishes, and mammals, without neglecting the islands
surveyed and their exotic, and sometimes, cannibalistic inhabitants. A large
number of these remarkable South Sea drawings are now reunited at the
Philosophical Society. In addition, after the *Peacock's* wreck in the mouth
of the Columbia River, Peale, at least was able to review and record the
Oregon species of Lewis and Clark (so badly preserved at the family's
museum) on an overland trek to the California coast.

After the expedition's return in 1842, all sources indicate that Peale's
professional standing was marred by his dispute with Lt Wilkes, the expedition's commander.[42] In 1846 Peale was removed from the payroll of the
official scientific corps. Subsequently, the zoological report on which he had
labored for four years was suppressed after an inadequate edition of one
hundred copies, and an outside expert's evaluation of his findings was
substituted and issued with Peale's magnificent *Atlas* drawings.[43] Peale was
understandably bitter about this treatment, and he never fully recovered from
the defeat. Because so many of his specimens were lost, his real contributions

to Pacific zoology have been extremely difficult to ascertain.[44] The new Peale materials are helpful here for they include drawings which are not found in the expedition's *Atlas*, and on study, may prove to be unique records of the valuable lost specimens Titian lamented in his letter to Franklin Peale. In addition, some of these annotated drawings depict ornithological specimens from the Wilkes Expedition which have been preserved in the Philadelphia Academy's collections, so that it is now possible to reunite drawings with the very specimens they record, and thus to re-evaluate Peale's scientific work in a precise way. For example, comparison of the new collection with the *Atlas* plates shows that Peale included drawings of the mule deer and South American wolf made before the Wilkes Expedition. Although Peale had lost many records on the expedition and was working under great pressure to complete the *Atlas*, such substitutions are not in the strictest tradition of scientific accuracy. Perhaps we can now view with more understanding Wilkes's growing dissatisfaction with Peale's methodology.

A second source is the journal of William L. Hudson owned by the American Museum of Natural History.[45] A veteran naval officer, Hudson was later in charge of laying down the first trans-Atlantic telegraph cable in 1857. In contrast to Hick's Utopian paintings, Hudson's journal offers a wry lay perspective on the value of scientific accomplishment, particularly Peale's, and many entries describe the mounting tensions between Wilkes, the scientific corps and the naval officers of the expedition. Throughout his journal, Captain Hudson deplored the hasty and shabby government outfitting of the expedition squadron.[46] The brig *Peacock* leaked so badly, that at one point, the carpet in Hudson's cabin was afloat![47] Indeed, Hudson reported with some relief that deep in Antarctic waters, the ship completely encased by ice, was at last dry:

> our Gun deck within the last thirty Hours—has been made quite tight-... by a natural caulker who has paid his work over with a coat of stuff some inches thick, and not in the careless manner of some Caulkers I could name (but forbear) who but *half pay their seams*—Our *Antarctic* Caulker has so thoroughly performed his duty that we shall be comparatively dry below—at least until a change of Temperature Strips off the *Peacocks Great Coat*—and with the aid of the Sun leaves us quite as unfitted for our perigrinations in this Climate—as the gaudy Bird whose name we bear.[48]

Hudson, like Peale, was also troubled by the high cost to taxpayers of the scientific expedition and the slackened naval discipline.[49] He described one crew member who managed to remain on the sick list as one of "Uncle Sam's hard bargains",[50] and at the halfway mark, he expressed his own frustrations with both the politics and the scientific pretentions of the long sea voyage:

> Nor am I yet prepared to allow that cruising amongst Icebergs, in *Thick Hazy* weather—when you have them popping up suddenly in your face to bid you defiance—and that without any previous notice—to be quite so agreeable—as being seated, *tete a tete*, at your own fireside—This fancy kind of sailing, *is not all* that it is *cracked up to be*.[51]

Cruising in warmer waters proved to be no safer. Claiming that the squadron floated off uncharted coral reefs only by the graces of Isaac Newton and Jim Crow, Hudson added this entry in April 1841:

> We have an exceedingly—dark—dirty—unpleasant night—and hardly know what reef—or coral patch—we may be thumping on—before we can see it—however, I've said enough—as some of the gentry at home, who of course know all about—have told the world through the public prints—"the Exploring Expedition was only a party of pleasure."[52]

For the most part, however, Hudson endured the difficult voyage with surprisingly good humor. In October 1840, he described the rising protein level of the rations at the Sandwich Islands:

> My coffee and sugar had given out—and what bread we had on board was litterally [sic] alive—my steward was in the habit of having my allowance well soaked in water—to keep it on the plate—and as he said— [to] prevent the worms from running off with it.[53]

A religious man, who Peale noted routinely put the crew through arduous Sunday services,[54] Hudson slyly regarded the impact of missionary zeal upon the native physique of the principal chief of the De Peyster's Islanders: "He was a fine looking man some 40 or 45 years of age grave in his deportment and his general appearance indicated that he got his full share of the loaves and fishes."[55] Hudson certainly had an observing eye. He also had a good ear for the apparent trivia of the interminable natural history debates surrounding the origin of species in the New World and the biblical significance of massive American fossils like the Mastodon exhibited at Peale's Museum:

> Mr Peale our naturalist while on the Bows first this morning watching for Fish observed approaching us from ahead *Two large* Quids of Tobacco a piece of Oakum and a small patch of Chips... so far as the Chips and Oakum are concerned it may have been from the Vessel of any nation— But the *Two Quids* or *Chews of Tobacco*—are quite another matter—and would seem to call in requisition the aid of my considering Cap—... I answer if they had been *small*—or of the *ordinary size* or *but one Quid*— we might fairly they had [been thrown from a Merchant Vessel]—But they were Mammoth Quids—a mouthful each.[56]

Therefore, Hudson concluded that the quids had been disgorged from the mouth of some seaman belonging to an American man of war. Although Hudson made jokes at Peale's expense, the naturalist's scientific enthusiasm was contagious, and the captain soon found himself attempting to identify seabirds.

While the humorous passages in Hudson's journal suggest that he was writing for an audience, Hudson apparently did not intend to publish this account. Despite the detailed meteorological data, this journal was not turned over to Wilkes for inclusion in the expedition's official narrative.[57] The reasons for Hudson's withholding are puzzling for Hudson did not share Peale's growing animus for Lt Wilkes. To the contrary, Hudson became increasingly respectful of the younger officer's leadership, and his journal is of particular interest because it records a number of incidents between Wilkes and the scientific corps not included in either Wilkes's official narrative or Peale's manuscript account. For example, it becomes evident that within the first six months of the expedition considerable friction was already developing among Wilkes, the naval officers, and the scientific "Gentlemen":

> This morning the Scientific Corps of Civilians were brought together by Signal on Board the Vincennes—after they had assembled in the Cabin— Capt Wilkes stated that he was fearful from what had unofficially reached his ears—there was reason to anticipate difficulties by party collisions— amongst themselves—as well as with some of them, and the officers—he had taken this early occasion of calling them to prevent so unpleasant an occurence—and to let them have a perfect understanding as to their relative positions in the Squadron... He assured them at the same time of all the protection and courtesy within the scope of his duty as Commander of the Squadron—and his great desire to aid and facilitate the operations of each and every individual of the Corps to the extent of his power—and he hoped they felt satisfied.[58]

At this point, the most vocal, dissatisfied member of the Scientific Corps was not Peale, but Joseph Pitty Couthouy (1808–1864), a young amateur conchologist from Boston:

> Mr Couthouy here stated that some of the officers had not been as prompt in aiding *him particularly* as he could have wished, and earnestly desired— he however hoped, and presumed he would have no further cause of complaint on that score—after half an hours conversation in which the Gentleman expressed a perfect coincidence of opinion in relation to a good understanding between themselves and the officers... the meeting broke up.

Neither Wilkes nor Peale refers to this confrontation, although Peale continued to mention petty rudenesses on the part of Lieutenant William M. Walker.[59]

Wilkes's omissions in the published account are understandable. Given his true feelings, Peale's lack of candor, perhaps, can be best explained by the fact that Wilkes had access to the journals kept by the officers and scientists. In the autumn of 1839, Wilkes apparently read some of the journals. Hudson described the meeting which followed:

> I was present this morning November 4th [1839] in the cabin of the Vincennes with Mr Carr—Doctor Gilchrist—Mr Dana and Mr Couthouy— this meeting occurred in consequence of some remarks which appeared in the journal of Mr Couthouy reprehending the official acts of Capt. Wilkes—which remarks he had read to different officers—previous to submitting them to his commander.[60]

Disclaiming any intention of disrespect for Wilkes, Couthouy did restate that certain orders issued by Wilkes in relation to specimens for the government had militated against the collections and that some of the officers, namely William May, had declared they would make no further collections. Wilkes warned Couthouy with dismissal in no uncertain terms and called in May, the son of President Washington's personal physician. The young surgeon "in a state of some excitement" denied Couthouy's claims, and not surprisingly, Wilkes eventually dismissed the industrious and idealistic conchologist later in the voyage.

Couthouy sailed with the *Vincennes* so that Peale on the *Peacock* was apparently unaware of the full extent of the younger man's tribulations with Wilkes. In his journal, Peale only mentions Couthouy's name four times in personnel lists, noting in one the latter's declining health. At best, Wilkes seemed to have viewed Couthouy (who was, interestingly enough, himself a merchant ship captain) as an amateur collector whose contributions to natural history ranked as those of a hobby. Despite his considerable experience, Peale, too, was self-taught, and Couthouy's demise included all the elements of his own. As in the case of Peale, an outside expert who had not accompanied the expedition was selected to describe Couthouy's collections and to submit the official government report. Because his scientific collections were mismanaged, Couthouy's contributions, too, will probably forever remain undefined by historians.

The ambiguities and contradictions Peale's lifework presents will continue to challenge students of American science. His achievements exemplify the prodigious and visually elegant accomplishments possible during the mid-nineteenth century, and his failures reveal the professional strictures of a rapidly emerging scientific community much larger than the Philadelphia-based natural history tradition which had shaped Peale's career goals. These little known bibliographic sources, Titian's new drawings and Hudson's Journal, suggest the great popular appeal and outreach of American natural history beyond Audubon's success into such surprising areas as folk painting. At the same time, these sources witness the scientific rejection of the distinctive approach to the Book of Nature which the Peale family did so much to promulgate in Philadelphia circles.

Ironically, while Peale bitterly complained during the 1840s that the government engravers were not doing justice to his *Atlas* illustrations, the aging Hicks was clumsily reworking versions of Titian's earlier Long Expedition drawings. Indeed, Peale himself returned to these early field studies, and the new group of drawings at the American Philosophical Society includes a number of tracings intended for large-scale oil compositions of bison, elk, and other western themes. The pursuits of Peale's final years were primarily artistic, although he tried without success to sell his valuable Lepidoptera collections to the U.S. Department of Agriculture.[61] Despite his physical retirement, the field naturalist did not relinquish his visual investigation of nature, and showing his father's fascination with technological inventions, Titian Peale took up photography in his old age.[62]

NOTES AND REFERENCES

[1] For a good introduction see Antonia McLean, 1972 *Humanisation and the Rise of Science in Tudor England* (New York: Neale Watson Academic Pub., Inc.: 22–27; 210–224.

[2] See the first ticket to the Museum illustrated in Charles Coleman Sellers, 1980 *Mr. Peale's Museum* (New York: W. W. Norton & Co., Inc.): 37; also shown by Raphael Peale, A Deception, india ink and pencil on paper, 1802, Kennedy Galleries, Inc., New York.

[3] See also, Patsy A. Gerstner, 1976 The Academy of Natural Sciences of Philadelphia, 1812–1850, in Alexandra Oleson and Sanborn C. Brown, eds., *The Pursuit of Knowledge in the Early American Republic* (Baltimore: Johns Hopkins University Press): 174–193.

[4] The ramifications of Wilson's influence are the subject of Charlotte M. Porter, 1979 The Concussion of Revolution: Publications and Reform at the early Academy of Natural Sciences, Philadelphia, 1812–1842, *Journal of the History of Biology* **12**: 273–292.

[5] For examples of such aspirations, see Harry B. Weiss and Grace M. Ziegler, 1931 *Thomas Say, Early American Naturalist* (Baltimore: Charles C. Thomas): 36–39; C. S. Rafinesque to George Ord, Oct. 1, 1817, T. J. Fitzpatrick Collection, Spencer Library, Kansas University, Lawrence.

[6] These are discussed by Charlotte M. Porter, 1979 'Subsilentio': Discouraged Works of early Nineteenth-Century American Natural History, *Journal of the Society for the Bibliography of Natural History* **9**: 109–119.

[7] Arnold Mallis, 1971 *American Entomologists* (New Brunswick: Rutgers University Press, 1841): 22–23; Asa Gray, 1841 Notice of the Botanical Writings of the late C. S. Rafinesque, *American Journal of Science* **40**: 221–241.

[8] Little has been published about Lieutenant Hudson, although his family papers have recently been deposited with the Library of Congress.

[9] "Journal II," 11 August 1840 to 19 February 1842, Southern Historical Collection, University of North Carolina, Chapel Hill.

[10] Titian Ramsay Peale to Franklin Peale, 30 October 1841, quoted by Jessie Poesch, 1961 *Titian Ramsay Peale* (Philadelphia: American Philosophical Society): 88.

[11] *Ibid.:* 95.

[12] T. Say, 1824, 1825, 1828 *American Entomology, or Descriptions of the Insects of North America,* 3 vols. (Philadelphia: Samuel Augustus Mitchell).

[13] Entomological Sketch Book, 1817, in original paper cover inscribed "Dr T. R. Peale 1106 Girard Street Philadelphia" and containing seventeen watercolor studies of metamorphosis. American Philosophical Society, Philadelphia.

[14] Peale was proposed for membership in the Academy on 26 November 1817, and he served as one of the minor officers off and on for the next fifteen years. After 1871, he was provided with a work room at the Academy, to which his entire collection of insects was bequeathed in 1899.

[15] See note 10; the Peale Family Papers are available on microfiche from the National Portrait Gallery, Smithsonian Institution, Washington, D.C.

[16] The significance of these expeditions is detailed by William H. Goetzmann, 1971 *Exploration and Empire* (New York: Alfred A. Knopf): 181–184; 233–239.

[17] Charles Willson Peale to Thomas Jefferson, 3 November 1805, Museum, in Donald Jackson, ed., 1962 *Letters of the Lewis and Clark Expedition with Related Documents* (Urbana: University of Illinois Press): 267; see also 308; 261; 272.

[18] The American Philosophical Society owns many of Titian's original drawings for Bonaparte's supplement to Wilson's *American Ornithology* (Philadelphia: Samuel Augustus Mitchell, 1825) vol. 1.

[19] Sellers, *Peale's Museum:* 248

[20] Edwin James, 1823 *Account of an Expedition from Pittsburgh to the Rocky Mountains Performed in the Years 1819, 1820* (London: Longman, Hurst, Rees, Orme and Brown): 354.

[21] For some reason, the *new* species were *not* included in Say's catalogue, but were briefly described in the footnotes in James's *Account.*

[22] John Davidson Godman, 1826 *American Natural History* (Philadelphia: H. C. Carey & I. Lea) **1**: vii.

[23] *Ibid.* 211–224, clearly demonstrates Godman's debt to the Museum, and the plate opposite page 204, the Great Mastodon by T. Peale, is after a Museum mount. See also Sellers, *Peale's Museum:* 39; 68; 104.

[24] Godman, *American Natural History:* vii; 80.

[25] For example, compare these plates in Godman, opposite pages 128 and 280 respectively, to Titian's drawings of the Missouri Bear and Wolf Lying on the Ground, American Philosophical Society.

[26] Poesch, *Titian Ramsay Peale:* 60

[27] Godman, *American Natural History:* 279.

[28] Stephanie Morris, 1974 John Davidson Godman (1974–1830) Physician and Naturalist, *Transactions and Studies of the College of Physicians of Philadelphia* **41:** 295-303.

[29] These are The Peaceable Kingdom, *ca* 1833, Albright-Knox Gallery; 1844, Abby Aldrich Rockefeller Folk Art Collection; and 1849, Galerie St. Etienne, New York.

[30] Hicks first use of the child is thought to be copied from an engraved illustration of a painting by Richard Westall which appeared in many Bibles in the United States; see *Hicks, Kane, Pippin* (Pittsburgh: Museum of Art, Carnegie Institute, 1966) unpaginated catalogue of the travelling exhibit.

[31] Hicks used the wolf and black bear in pictures before 1833, but these animals were not based upon American natural history models.

[32] Some of Titian Peale's western drawings of animals were exhibited at the Annual Exhibition of the Academy of Fine Arts in Philadelphia in 1822. However, it is more likely that Hicks saw Peale's Missouri Bears as a lithograph published in the *Cabinet of Natural History and American Rural Sports* in 1830. The *Cabinet,* published from 1830 to 1836 by the artists John and Thomas Doughty, was well known to the Philadelphia community of painters and included articles by George Catlin and others.

[33] For example, the leopard in Hick's earliest known composition of The Peaceable Kingdom, *ca* 1820, Cleveland Museum of Art, appears to be taken from Noah and His Ark, a painting by Charles Catton, copied in 1819 by Charles Willson Peale for exhibition in the Museum; see C. W. Peale to Titian, 25 December 1952 1819, quoted in Charles Coleman Sellers, *Transactions of the American Philosophical Society* **42:** 44-45.

[34] Originally published in the popular Philadelphia *Port Folio,* Wilson's epic verse, "The Foresters, Description of a Pedestrian Tour to the Fall of Niagara in the Autumn of 1804" is discussed in terms of its popular appeal by Hans Huth, 1957 *Nature and the American* (Berkeley: University of California Press; Bison Book reprint; 1972): 24-29.

[35] Alice Ford, 1952 *Edward Hicks; Painter of the Peaceable Kingdom* (Philadelphia: University of Pennsylvania): 33.

[36] Compare the illustration of the Cougar in Godman, *American Natural History* opposite page 297, presumably based upon a Museum mount, to Hicks's striped cat in The Peaceable Kingdom, *ca* 1835, Mrs Holger Cahill. A leopard and wild-cat were certainly on display by 1787 when they were recorded by the Rev. Manasseh Cutler; the sheriff's sale catalogue of the Museum also includes a mounted "Wolf and lamb group", C. C. Sellers, *Peale's Museum:* 27; 315.

[37] For example, see C. W. Peale's description of his young daughter feeding a fierce hyena in his *Scientific and Descriptive Catalogue of Peale's Museum* (Philadelphia: printed by Samuel H. Smith, 1796) and his letter to Rubens Peale, 19 August 1805, about young Titian: "The other day he brought home a ground Squirrel alive and the day before yesterday a field Mouse. He posses no fear to take hold of such animals alive, and says that he won't let them bite him." Letterbook No. 6: 139, American Philosophical Society.

[38] C. A. Browne, 1936 Some Relations of the New Harmony Movement to the History of Science in America, *Scientific Monthly* **42:** 492.

[39] William Maclure, 1825 Mr. Owen and his Plans of Educatoin, *American Journal of Science* **9:** 238.

[40] Edwin G. Conklin, 1940 Connection of the American Philosophical Society with Our First National Exploring Expedition, *Proceedings of the American Philosophical Society.* **82:** 530.

[41] Poesch, *Titian Ramsay Peale:* 139, Peale's entry for Monday, 25 February 1839 at Orange Harbor.

[42] *Ibid.:* 94-103; George Ord to T. R. Peale, 27 January 1852, Philadelphia, Misc. Ms Collection, American Philosophical Society.

[43] Titian furnished eight plates of mammals and twenty-four of birds for the official issue of the *Atlas, Mammalogy and Ornithology* by John Cassin, 1858 (Philadelphia: C. Sherman & Son, printers) or thirty-two of the total fifty-three plates. Four mammal plates and twenty-seven bird plates contemplated by Peale were suppressed and may be represented by drawings in the new APS acquisition.

[44] Harley Harris Bartlett, 1940 The Reports of the Wilkes Expedition, and the Work of the Specialists in Science, *Proceedings of the American Philosophical Society.* **82:** 642–646.

[45] The Museum's manuscript journal is the gift of Ivor B. Clark, a grandson of William L. Hudson.

[46] See, for examples, W. L. Hudson, Journal, vol. 1, p. 5; 8; 9; 21; 87–88.

[47] See also pages 132; 135; 150; 156.

[48] *Ibid.,* p. 153.

[49] See Titian Peale, The South Seas Surveying and Exploring Expedition: Its Organization, Equipment, Purposes, Results, and Termination, page 10, Titian Ramsay Peale Papers, American Museum of Natural History.

[50] W. L. Hudson, Journal, vol. 2, page 32, (microfilm copy, American Museum of Natural History).

[51] *Ibid.,* p. 151.

[52] *Ibid.,* p. 223, entry for April 19.

[53] *Ibid.,* vol. 2, p. 38.

[54] Poesch, *Titian Ramsay Peale:* 130, Titian's entry for Sunday, 7 October 1838.

[55] Hudson, Journal, vol. 2, p. 163, entry for 18 March 1841.

[56] *Ibid.,* vol. 1, pp. 64–65, entry for 5 November 1838.

[57] Hudson's Journal is not included in the definitive bibliography by Daniel C. Haskell, 1942 *The United States Exploring Expedition, 1838–1842, and its Publications* (New York: New York Public Library). Although Wilkes selected most of the meteorological equipment for the expedition, the planned volume XXIV on physics never materialized.

[58] Hudson, Journal, vol. 1, pp. 98–99, entry for 1 January 1839.

[59] Compare Hudson's account to Charles Wilkes, *Narrative of the United States Exploring Expedition,* vol. 1 (New York: G. P. Putnam & Co., 1856): 88–89, and Poesch, *Titian Ramsay Peale:* 169, Titian's entry for Sunday, 3 May 1840.

[60] Hudson, Journal, vol. 1, pp. 328–329, entry for 26 November 1839. Again, Wilkes only mentions a "private interview" with Hudson; see *Narrative,* vol. 2, p. 90.

[61] See C. V. Riley to Spencer Baird, 15 November 1884, Smithsonian Archives, Record Unit 139, Box No. 1, p. 264. Riley considered Peale's asking price of $550 to be "very low", but the collection was not purchased.

[62] His photographs have been recently displayed at the Library of George Washington University, Washington, D.C.

HUDSON'S BAY COMPANY ARCHIVES 1670–1870: A REFERENCE SOURCE FOR NATURAL HISTORIANS

Shirlee Anne Smith
Keeper, Hudson's Bay Company Archives,
Provincial Archives of Manitoba,
Department of Cultural Affairs and Historical Resources,
200 Vaughan Street,
Winnipeg,
Manitoba, R3C OV8,
Canada

The Archives Department of the Hudson's Bay Company was not established until 1924,[1] although North Americans were admitted to the records during the early years of this century. As occasionally happens in Canadian affairs American historians, especially those from the State of Oregon, seemed to be more interested in the records than their British or Canadian counterparts.[2] Considering, however, the roles played by such Company men as John McLoughlin and Peter Skene Ogden in the affairs of the North Pacific States such interest is readily understandable.

The records to be identified, sorted, arranged and classified extended over 250 years. It was a daunting task for the Archivist and his staff. Advice was sought and generously given by officials from the Public Record Office, London. With minor changes the recommendations were implemented. For the first two hundred years the records created by the Company remained fairly consistent. Such consistency and continuity greatly aided the Archives staff in the sorting, arranging and classifying. On the whole the organizational methods have worn well. This statement is based on the premise that the test of a good classification system is how quickly and easily it can be understood by researchers. The Archives are not complete. The deficit in the Seventeenth century may be owing to the fact that the Adventurers met in coffee houses, or in each other's lodgings. This lack of a permanent home could not have made record keeping an easy matter. Undoubtedly, too, many records were destroyed, while others were consumed by fire, or lost in canoeing or shipping accidents. Despite these problems the material under review measures approximately 2,500 linear feet.

As the Hudson's Bay Company is the oldest chartered trading Company in the world its records relating to native history and environmental studies in the Canadian pre-Confederation period are unparalleled. For a number of places in Canada, many of them native Indian communities, the Archives has the only documentation for the eighteenth and nineteenth centuries; and for the eighteenth century, in particular, there are continuous daily records thus enabling researchers to compile long range data.

Contributions to the History of North American Natural History. Society for the Bibliography of Natural History, London, 1983.

For the purposes of classification the Archives are divided into eight main Sections:

Section A —London operations
     B —North American operations
     C —Shipping
     D —Papers of Overseas Governor, i.e., North America
     E —Records relating to the Company but not created by it, for example, personal diaries
     F —Subsidiary companies
     G —Maps
     Z —Miscellaneous.[3]

Section A, the records originating in London, are of interest to those researchers seeking details on policy matters and the produce sold. Except for the years 1670–71, 1675–1678, all the Minute Books have survived and, starting in 1679, there is a continuous series of Letters Outward to the Officers in North America. As the Company's main business was the trade in furs one must turn to the Fur Sales Books and the Fur Sales Catalogues for information on the kinds of furs, and the other items including castoreum, feathers, quills and isinglass sold at the London auctions.

The trading post records, Section B, is sub-divided into classes: Journals, Correspondence Inward and Outward, Accounts, Reports and miscellaneous. For the first 200 years of the Company's operations there are daily journals for approximately 210 posts, extending from North West River in Labrador to Victoria on Vancouver Island, and from the Arctic Circle to the Snake River expeditions in the northern Pacific States. The correspondence in this section is generally between posts and gives the researcher an insight into the relationships between officers, and officers and servants. The account books have received scant attention, with the exception of the painstaking and original work done by Professor Arthur Ray.[4] These are kept in pounds, shillings, and pence and contain lists of goods traded, the prices in Made-Beaver, and the accounts of the Officers, Servants and Indians. Over 5,000 Account Books have survived and this figure includes almost 1,300 for York Factory, the Headquarters of the large Northern Department. The annual reports on trade consist of geographical descriptions of the country, the kinds of animals inhabiting it, the number of hunters, and the amount of rations provided for Company employees. The inevitable miscellaneous contains some unusual items, including marriage contracts, citations of divorce, lists of medicines and Indian vocabularies.

The earliest ship's log dates from 1751 and for many voyages there are duplicates, one kept by the Master and one by the First Mate. These duplicates are invariably a bonus for researchers as it gives them an opportunity to cross-check data. The 1,070 ships' logs are not in a particularly good state of repair. Considering the conditions under which these records were created this is not surprising. The long voyage, by sail, from London around The Horn to the Columbia River generally took about seven months. The voyage to Hudson Bay, by comparison, was less than three months.[5]

The papers of Sir George Simpson, Governor of the Company's trading territories, in D. Section, are one of the most important blocks of correspondence for the nineteenth century. As the Company's chief representative his correspondence with Company officers, and with religious and political leaders, are a useful source for studying events in British North America for the period 1821–1860. He had an unrivalled knowledge of the country and its personalities, and his lengthy annual reports to the Governor and Committee in London show his grasp of detail and his business acumen.

Some of the most interesting and less usual items are classified in Section E. These consist of Baptisms, Marriages, and Burials for the Red River Settlement; census reports, the Peter Fidler journals of mapping and exploration, and the 'Observations' of James Isham and Andrew Graham. Isham's Observations were written in 1743 at Prince of Wales's Fort in present-day Manitoba and give detailed accounts of the customs of Indians and the flora and fauna. Graham spent most of his career on the West Coast of Hudson Bay where he compiled his journals on mammals, birds, reptiles, fishes, insects, Indians and Eskimos. The works of both these men have been published by the Hudson's Bay Record Society.[6]

The records of the Puget's Sound Agricultural Company and the North West Company are in Section F. The PSAC operated farms south of the 49th parallel in what is today the State of Washington. There are surprisingly few records of the North West Company in the Archives. Generally, it is more rewarding to consult the Hudson's Bay Company daily journals for information on the Nor'Westers, particularly on their trading operations.

Fur traders surveyed and mapped large areas of North America. Philip Turnor, David Thompson and Peter Fidler mapped much of Western Canada, while James Clouston explored and mapped various areas in Quebec. With the exception of the work of David Thompson these manuscript maps have survived in the Archives. One of Clouston's maps shows an area which was still shown as unmapped on the Canadian Government National Topographic Sheet 32, N.E. Mistassini, 1953.[7]

The Z Section is a mélange containing papers of the Third Duke of Buckingham and Chandos; and Deeds referring to land in Stapleford Abbots, England.

Considering that the Company's main business was to trade goods for furs and skins it is not surprising that there are numerous references in the Archives to natural history. One of the most important archival sources for this information is the daily journals of events which every post factor was obliged to keep. In 1683, the London Committee informed their officers on Hudson Bay that they required to be kept "Journalls of what hath been done in the respective factories & of all occurrances that have happened to them the yeare past".[8] In 1814 the Committee was more explicit and exhorted the officers to include a "description of navigation, nature of the country, the climate, details of post buildings, ground under cultivation, particulars regarding Company employees, Indians and the "Canadians" and of the trade".[9] In a large measure the journals were kept in a good hand, and contained the information requested by London.

The Company's post at Churchill in modern Manitoba provides a good example of the kind of research that can be achieved from daily journals. The journals date from the establishment of Churchill in 1717 without a break until 1867, except for the year 1782 when Comte de la Pérouse shelled the Fort and took the men prisoner. They record the temperature, wind, snowfall, rainfall, break-up and freeze-up of the river, the sighting of the first geese, the number of Indians who came to trade, the condition of the winter's hunt, the employment of the servants, and other details. One can trace the effect of the environment on the animals and people, which in turn affected the fortunes of the Hudson's Bay Company. When the snow was heavy large game found it difficult to move about in search of food and were an easy prey for the Indians. Conversely, when the weather was frigid and the days short the Indians found it difficult to hunt the animals. When this happened they crowded into the Company post as many as 78 at a time [10] where the factor gave them oatmeal for sustenance. All these events of daily living provide information on animal habitats and cycles, country provisions, diet, climate change, the customs of the Indians, and the relationship between Indians and Europeans.

In addition to the journal of events there are also journals of travel and exploration. The number surviving in the Company's Archives is not as great as might be expected, when the number of men who made exploratory journeys is taken into account. However, it must be remembered that some of these inland travellers, though quite able to look after themselves and communicate with the Indians in their own dialects were frequently illiterate. Often it is from these first inland travels that the most vivid descriptions of flora, fauna, native peoples and the territory are recorded. James Sutherland in 1796 when travelling for the first time from his post north of Lake Superior to the Western Prairies wrote in his journal that he "travel'd all day through beautiful plains which only wants the hand of industry to make this one of the finest countries in the universe no clearing of ground wanted, but the plow to till".[11] It was a prophetic statement. The Archives has some, but not all the journals of the travels of Alexander Ross, Peter Skene Ogden, William Kittson and John Work in the American West, and those of Samuel Hearne, and Peter Fidler, in the Canadian West.

In addition to providing information on the various branches of natural history, the Archives also contains references to various collections. Shortly after its incorporation, the Company started its long collaboration with the Royal Societies in London and Edinburgh,[12] and later the Smithsonian Institution in Washington. The 1770s was a prolific period for the London Royal Society when boxes of stuffed and dried skins of quadrupeds and birds were received from the men on Hudson Bay. Joseph Henry, Secretary of the Smithsonian Institution, who has been described as "the most distinguished American scientist of the 19th century",[13] asked Governor George Simpson in 1857 for assistance in acquiring musk ox, barren ground reindeer and mountain goat.[14] The Company readily agreed and some of the work was carried out by the celebrated naturalist Robert Kennicott.[15]

Since the transfer of the Archives from London, England, to Winnipeg, Manitoba, in 1974, there has been a notable increase in the number of research visits; the subjects consulted cover the various branches of natural history. Anthropologists, botanists, environmentalists, historical geographers, and zoologists search for evidence of previous native cultures, climatic fluctuations, and changes in flora and fauna. With increased research their findings will become more scientific and less inferential which is, after all, what scholarship and archives are all about.

NOTES AND REFERENCES

[1] Hudson's Bay Company Archives (hereinafter referred to as HBCA) A.1/167, fo. 134. See also Joan Craig,1970 Three Hundred Years of Records, *The Beaver*: 65-70.

[2] Agnes C. Laut had access to the records in 1905-06 and Professor Frederick Merck at a later date. E. E. Rich, (ed.) 1950 *Peter Skene Ogden's Snake Country Journals 1824-25 and 1825-26,* (London: The Hudson's Bay Record Society, Vol. XIII): vii. Professor R. C. Clark, and Dr Burt Brown Barker, University of Oregon both requested access to the Archives before they were officially opened to the public. (Archives V.F. Oregon — Burt Brown Barker and R. C. Clark.)

[3] There are individual catalogues for each section.

[4] See Arthur J. Ray, The early Hudson's Bay Company Account Books as Sources for Historical Research: An Analysis and Assessment, *Archivaria,* 1(1), Winter 1975-76: 3-38. Arthur J. Ray and Donald B. Freeman, 1978 *Give us Good Measure: An Economic Analysis of Relations Between the Indians and the Hudson's Bay Company Before 1763,* (Toronto: The University of Toronto Press.

[5] The barque Columbia left Gravesend on 23 August 1835 and arrived at Fort Vancouver on the Columbia River on 10 April, 1836, HBCA C.1/243. The Prince of Wales left Gravesend on 6 June 1836 and arrived at Moose Factory at the Bottom of James Bay on 2 September 1836, HBCA C.1/830.

[6] E. E. Rich, A. M. Johnson, (eds), 1949 *James Isham's Observations on Hudson's Bay, 1743,* (Toronto, Published by the Champlain Society for the Hudson's Bay Record Society); Glyndwr Williams, (ed.), *Andrew Graham's Observations on Hudson's Bay 1767-91,* (London: The Hudson's Bay Record Society).

[7] Clouston's map is HBCA B.133/e/1. See also Glyndwr Williams, 1966 James Clouston's Journey, *The Beaver*: 4-15; D. W. Moodie and Barry Kaye, 1977 'The Ac Ko Mok Ki Map', *The Beaver*: 4-15; J. G. MacGregor, 1966 *Peter Fidler: Canada's Forgotten Surveyor, 1769-1822,* (Toronto: McClelland and Stewart).

[8] E. E. Rich, A. M. Johnson (eds.), 1948 *Copy—Book of Letters Outward &c 1679-1687,* (Toronto: Published by The Champlain Society for the Hudson's Bay Record Society): 73.

[9] Joan Craig, 1970 Three Hundred Years of Records, *The Beaver*: 67-68.

[10] Ferdinand Jacobs wrote in the York Factory Journal: "I have now 78 Indians at the Factory to support not one of them can I get to go from the Factory to Provide for themselves for fear of being starved till the days are a little longer." HBCA B.239/a/65, fo.16.

[11] HBCA B.22/a/4, fo.10d.

[12] See R. P. Stearns, 1945 The Royal Society and the Company, *The Beaver*: 8-13.

[13] Letter from Whitfield J. Bell, Jr., librarian, American Philosophical Society, Philadelphia, dated 9 July 1968, to R. A. Reynolds, Secretary, Hudson's Bay Company, London.

[14] HBCA D.5/45, fo.265d.

[15] See Grace Lee Nute, 1943 Kennicott in the North, *The Beaver*: 28-32.

COMPILING AMERICAN GEOLOGICAL LITERATURE, 1669 TO 1850: A SYSTEMATIC APPROACH TO NATURAL HISTORY BIBLIOGRAPHY

Robert M. Hazen, Margaret Hindle Hazen, and Larry W. Finger
Geophysical Laboratory,
Carnegie Institution of Washington,
Washington, DC 20008

INTRODUCTION

The need for comprehensive and accurate bibliographies in the natural sciences is obvious. As a result of a combination of recently published library reference aids, microfilm reproductions of rare sources, and new word-processing capabilities, the production of systematic historical bibliographies is far easier than it was in the past.

From 1971 to 1980 we compiled and revised a geological bibliography of pre-1851 American-published sources (Hazen and Hazen, 1980). The objective of this review is to document our systematic approach to producing *American Geological Literature* in order to aid and encourage others engaged in bibliographic efforts. In addition, we highlight some of the advantages of word processing in the production of a bibliography.

DEFINING THE CONTENT

The first step in compiling a bibliography is to define the scope of the work. There is no simple solution to this problem, and each bibliographer must carefully consider his time and interests. In general, the broader the scope, the longer and possibly less comprehensive the result will be.

In *American Geological Literature,* we wished to produce a bibliography primarily for the use of historians of American natural science. We define geology in its broadest sense; references include both descriptive and analytical accounts of earth materials from all countries, geological processes and events, and mining and related economic pursuits. Several previously published earth-science bibliographies contain substantial numbers of historical references, but, in general, these works list only significant scientific articles or books. Thousands of other publications, including pamphlets on mining, book reviews of geology texts, notices of transient phenomena such as earthquakes and volcanoes, and accounts of geologists and their work, had never been cataloged. Additional unrecorded publications, including eighteenth century earthquake sermons, popular accounts of natural disasters, mining company stockholders' reports, and geological poetry, have little formal scientific content, yet are important to the historian as documents of the varied ways in which man viewed the earth. We sought to list all these geological publications. Unfortunately, it was necessary to omit newspaper

Contributions to the History of North American Natural History. Society for the Bibliography of Natural History, London, 1983.

articles from the bibliography because examination of the more than two million American newspaper issues published through 1850 was impossible.

Only American-published works were included. Many important European periodicals were not available to us, and any attempt to compile a list of foreign-published material would have fallen far short of a complete record. Of course, foreign texts and articles captured the attention of American scientists. As a consequence many of these works were abstracted, reviewed, or even republished in the United States and thus appear in the bibliography.

The bibliography was limited to sources published before 1851 for reasons of time and space. The extension of the work through 1860 would have doubled the number of entries (Hazen, 1980).

COMPILATION PROCEDURES

The bibliography was compiled from three main groups of sources: previously published bibliographies, periodicals, and library catalogs. As a first step a "core" list of references was compiled from existing geological and related bibliographies (of which there are more than eighty). Foremost among these tools are the well-known compilations of Darton (1896), Nickles (1923), Meisel (1924–1927), and Pestana (1972). Other more specialized bibliographies on the geology of most states, on specific geological phenomena, or of a specific author, supplemented the initial list. Of course, catalogs of historical imprints by Bristol (1970), Evans (1903–1934), Sabin (1961), Shaw and Shoemaker (1958–1965), Shipton (1955), and Shoemaker (1964–) were valuable in identifying early geological publications. Approximately 4,000 references were found in previously published bibliographies, and these entries comprised the core list.

Among the core references fewer than fifty different American-published periodicals were cited. To ensure that additional periodicals containing geological literature were not omitted, we conducted a search of the *Union List of Serials* (Titus, 1965), and all pre-1851 journals were noted. More than 2,000 titles were found, and although more than half of these were extremely rare and unavailable in complete runs, nearly 1,000 complete early American journals were to be found in American libraries. Of the complete runs, approximately 700 were accessible to us, many through the *American Periodical Microfilm Series* (Xerox University Microfilms, 1975). Included in the 700 titles were all major popular, literary, review, scientific, juvenile, eclectic, agricultural, medical, military, mining, mechanical, and religious periodicals published in the United States through 1850. Each of these journal runs was examined page by page for all earth-science notes, articles, and reviews. Journal sources added almost 10,000 references to the core list.

The list of 14,000 references was further expanded by entries found during a search of the Library of Congress printed catalogs and the card catalogs of selected research libraries. The most comprehensive source is the *National Union Catalog* (Mansell, 1968–1980). All entries on an author list, compiled from all book and article authors in the list of 14,000 references, were searched in Mansell for additional entries. In addition, the card catalog of the Baker Library of the Harvard Business School provided a source for mining and railroad company reports. Almost 1,000 book and pamphlet references were added through systematic searching of these library catalogs.

In an effort to conserve space in the final publication, the approximately 15,000 references were consolidated to 11,133 entries in three ways. Books that had multiple printings, or in some cases multiple editions, were listed under a single entry. Journal articles that appeared in two or more different periodicals were listed under a single numbered entry. Finally, dozens of short one- to nine-line notices on similar topics from a given periodical (e.g., notes on mining in *Niles' Weekly Register* or notes on volcanoes in *Scientific American*) were combined and listed as single entries.

The bibliography is still incomplete for several types of published sources. Perhaps the least complete portion is the listing of mining and railroad company publications (share advertisements, stockholders' reports, mine geology reports, articles of incorporation, and bylaws), which must have been published for many of the hundreds of operating mines in the United States. Only about 300 mining imprints were found in our search, and it is anticipated that many more will be found by other researchers. It is also to be expected that other earth-science articles will be found in the 1,300 periodicals not examined by us. However, we have included all scientific journals, and most of the omitted titles had only one or two volumes published. Therefore, it seems certain that the great majority of such articles have been listed.

ORGANIZATION AND PRESENTATION

The gathering of references is more than half the bibliographer's battle. The remaining tasks—organization and presentation—have been made vastly easier since the advent of word processing. The first, and most time-consuming, step in preparing a list of references for publication is the clerical operation of typing the entries into magnetic storage (usually a magnetic diskette). It is desirable to select a consistent set of abbreviations for periodical titles before typing the reference list. This reference list must be proofread with extreme care, but this is the last time the proofreading needs to be done. When the typing is complete it is a simple matter to arrange the references automatically, whether alphabetically by author, chronologically, by place of imprint, or in other ways with a word-processing system. The entire file of references, which was typed in arbitrary order, may thus be arranged in a preferred sequence. Additional information, such as author dates, can be added manually.

It is desirable, for ease in handling cross-references and for use in indexing (see below), to assign each reference a consecutive number. It is possible to assign these numbers automatically after the reference file is in its final sequence. Thus, there will be no errors in numbering from the first through the final entry.

In the final step before printing the bibliography the references must be transformed into an easy-to-read format. We prefer an arrangement in which the references are listed alphabetically by author, then chronologically within each author entry, with the reference number, author, and date each appearing in a separate set of columns. This format is easy to read, and specific reference numbers, authors, or years may be located rapidly.

Modern letter-quality printers produce high-quality copy that is suitable for direct transfer to printing plates. *American Geological Literature*, for example, was produced in this fast and inexpensive way. The number of characters per line and lines per inch must be carefully scaled to ensure efficient use of the printed page without loss of legibility. A print density of 18 characters per inch and 12 lines per inch is satisfactory for most reference works. Page numbers, alphabetic keys, or consecutive reference numbers can be added by the printer at the top of each page.

INDEXING

If the reference list is the heart of a bibliography, the index is its soul. Without an accurate and detailed index even the most comprehensive bibliography is of limited use to any but the most dedicated users. Word processing has facilitated the rapid and accurate indexing of bibliographies; time savings of 90% compared with manual indexing are typical. The following procedures constitute one method of "computerized" indexing.

The bibliographer must first assign key words or index terms to each reference. This information is typed into a master index file, which for each bibliographic entry contains the reference number followed by any desired number of key words. Consider, for example, a hypothetical reference number 1347, an article on gold mining in California with special emphasis on geological setting and mine safety. Index entries might include "California/ Gold Mining", "Gold Mining/California", "California/Geology", and "Mine Safety." The master index file entry for this article would appear as follows:

1347
California$Gold Mining
California/Geology
Mine Safety

The symbol "$" is used to indicate that both "California" and "Gold Mining" are to appear as main headings, with the other as subheading. The symbol "/" is used to indicate that only "California" is a main heading and "Geology" is the subheading. The use of "Mine Safety" alone indicates that there is no subheading. Typing of the master index file may be streamlined by substituting abbreviations for commonly used key words or phrases (e.g., "CF" for California or "GM" for Gold Mining). These abbreviations may be expanded automatically after the entire master index file has been typed. Proofreading of reference numbers is best done from the master index file. Each number appears only once, and numbers should be in consecutive order in this file.

The master index file, when complete, consists of a number and key words for each reference. The master file is transformed into final form in two

TABLE 1   Three steps in the production of indices with a word processing system. Hypothetical references 1347 through 1350 are given as examples.

STEP 1: Master Index File Typing this file into magnetic storage is the first step in production of an index.	STEP 2: Expanded Index File This file is in alphabetical order and is generated automatically from the master index file.	STEP 3: Final Index File This file, which is suitable for printing, is generated automatically from the expanded index file.

1347
California$Gold Mining
California/Geology
Mine Safety
1348
Massachusetts/Geology
Massachusetts$Geological
  Maps
Massachusetts$Coal Mining
1349
Mine Safety
Connecticut$Copper Mining
Connecticut$Coal Mining
1350
Granite$Russia
Building Stones/Granite
	Building Stones/Granite: 1350
	California/Geology: 1347
	California/Gold Mining: 1347
	Coal Mining/Connecticut:
	  1349
	Coal Mining/Massachusetts:
	  1348
	Connecticut/Coal Mining:
	  1349
	Connecticut/Copper Mining:
	  1349
	Copper Mining/Connecticut:
	  1349
	Geological Maps/
	  Massachusetts: 1348
	Gold Mining/California: 1347
	Granite/Russia: 1350
	Massachusetts/Coal Mining:
	  1348
	Massachusetts/Geological
	  Maps: 1348
	Massachusetts/Geology: 1348
	Mine Safety: 1347
	Mine Safety: 1349
	Russia/Granite: 1350
		Building Stones
		  Granite: 1350
		California
		  Geology: 1347
		  Gold Mining: 1347
		Coal Mining
		  Connecticut: 1349
		  Massachusetts: 1348
		Connecticut
		  Coal Mining: 1349
		  Copper Mining: 1349
		Copper Mining
		  Connecticut: 1349
		Geological Maps
		  Massachusetts: 1348
		Gold Mining
		  California: 1347
		Granite
		  Russia: 1350
		Massachusetts
		  Coal Mining: 1348
		  Geological Maps: 1348
		  Geology: 1348
		Mine Safety: 1347, 1349
		Russia
		  Granite: 1350

steps, as illustrated in Table 1. In the first step the file is automatically edited so that each separate index entry is expanded into full form and placed in alphabetical order. Thus, the three line entries for reference 1347 above now appear as four entries (heading/subheading:number) in correct order:

California/Geology:1347
California/Gold Mining:1347
Gold Mining/California:1347
Mine Safety:1347

At this point it is especially easy to proofread the index headings and subheadings for consistency of spelling and usage. This expanded index file, like any computer file, can be revised and edited by hand.

The final automatic editing procedure is the consolidation of all main headings and subheadings, with reference numbers following in numerical order (Table 1). Additional index information, such as *see* and *see also* entries, should be added to this file by hand. Like the main body of the bibliography, the final index file may be printed on a letter-quality machine for direct publication.

It should be emphasized that this indexing procedure completely eliminates the time-consuming and error-prone use of index cards. Proofreading is greatly simplified, and index typing and formating are completely automated. It should also be noted that this index procedure is equally applicable to books and manuscripts, where page numbers may be substituted for reference numbers.

CONCLUSIONS

The production of a bibliography has always been, and likely always will be, a time-consuming task. As a result of recently available library reference works and reproductions of rare eighteenth and nineteenth century sources, the bibliographer's task has been made significantly easier. Word processing has resulted in faster, more accurate, and more economical production of these bibliographies.

The production of a comprehensive bibliography for all aspects of American-published natural history through 1850 is certainly an obtainable goal. *American Geological Literature,* with 15,000 references, was completed in the equivalent of one-and-a-half years of work by one person, following procedures outlined above. A comprehensive bibliography of botany or zoology would probably contain no more than two to three times that number of entries, so the time scale of such an endeavor is not unreasonable. The rewards of such a project would more than repay the dedicated bibliographer.

REFERENCES

BRISTOL, R. P., 1970 *Supplement to Charles Evans' American Bibliography.* Charlottesville: University Press of Virginia, 636 p.

DARTON, N. H., 1896 Catalogue and index of contributions to North American geology, 1732–1891. *U.S. Geological Survey Bulletin* 127, 1045 p.

EVANS, C., 1903–1934 *American Bibliography.* Chicago: Blakely Press, 12 v.

HAZEN, R. M., 1980 Publication in American geology to 1850. *Journal of Geological Education* **28**:249–255.

HAZEN, R. M., and HAZEN M. H., 1980 *American Geological Literature, 1669 to 1850.* Stroudsburg, PA: Dowden, Hutchinson and Ross, Inc., 431 p.

MEISEL, M., 1924–1927 *A Bibliography of American Natural History.* New York: Premier Publishing Co., 3 v.

MANSELL [publisher], 1968–1980 *National Union Catalog: Pre—1956 Imprints.* London: Mansell, 680 v.

NICKLES, J. M., 1923 Geological Literature on North America, 1785—1918. *U.S. Geological Survey Bulletin* 746. 1167 p.

PESTANA, H. R., 1972 *Bibliography of Congressional Geology.* New York: Hafner Publishing Co., 285 p.

SABIN, J., 1961 *A Dictionary of Books Relating to America, from Its Discovery to the Present Time.* Amsterdam: N. Israel, 29 v.

SHAW, R. R., and SHOEMAKER R. H., 1958–1965 *American Bibliography: A Preliminary Checklist.* New York: Scarecrow Press, 19 v., Addenda.

SHIPTON, C. K., 1955 *Charles Evans' American Bibliography,* Volume 13. Worcester, Massachusetts: American Antiquarian Society.

SHOEMAKER, R. H., 1964 (continuing) *Checklist of American Imprints, 1820-*. New York: Scarecrow Press.

TITUS, E. B., ed., 1965 *Union List of Serials in Libraries of the United States and Canada,* 3rd edition. New York: H. W. Wilson, 5 v.

XEROX University Microfilms, 1975 *American Periodicals, 1700-1900: A Consolidated Bibliography.* Ann Arbor, MI:Xerox University Microfilms, 30 p.